BELLINGHAM PUBLIC LIBRARY
BELLINGHAM, WASHINGTON

MW00627510

THE STORY OF THE SECHELT NATION

DATE DUE

AUG 8 ▓▓▓		
MAY 1 7 1994		
JUL 7 1997		

DEMCO 38-296

THE STORY
of the
SECHELT NATION

by Lester Peterson

SECHELT INDIAN BAND

971.131
PETERSON

Copyright © 1990 by Lester Peterson

All rights reserved. No part of this book may be reproduced or transmitted in any form by any means without permission in writing from the publisher, except by a reviewer, who may quote brief passages in a review.

Published by
 Harbour Publishing
 Box 219
 Madeira Park, BC V0N 2H0
for the Sechelt Indian Band, Sechelt, BC

Cover design and photograph by Roger Handling
Map drawn by Roger Handling
Printed and bound in Canada

Canadian Cataloguing in Publication Data

Peterson, Lester R., 1917–
 The story of the Sechelt nation

 ISBN 1-55017-017-1 paper
 ISBN 1-55017-035-X cloth

 1. Sechelt Indians – History.*   2. Indians of North America – British Columbia – Sechelt Peninsula – History   3. Indians of North America – British Columbia – Jervis Inlet Region – History. I. Title.
E99.S21P48 1990   971.1'31   C90-091293-6

TRADITIONAL HOMESITES AND PICTOGRAPH
LOCATIONS OF THE SECHELT NATION

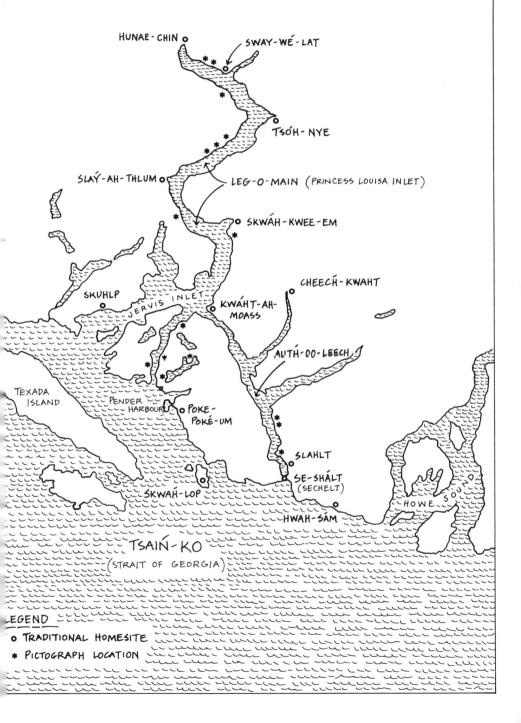

Preface

In 1923, my parents established a home at Gibson's Landing, on the western shore of Howe Sound. Near us, to the south, lay the Strait of Georgia, which, for some sixty miles upcoast from the 49th Parallel, separates Vancouver Island from the mainland of British Columbia.

Soon after our arrival, we learned that a small band of Native Indians known as the Sechelt lived fifteen miles away, on a narrow neck of land separating the end of Sechelt Inlet from the Strait. The children from this village attended Saint Augustine Residential School, operated there by the Oblate Order. Occasionally, I met some of the boys from this school at soccer games and track meets. All were destined eventually to work at fishing and logging, occupations that had been followed by their fathers, as well as mine.

In 1951, after some years away from my home community, I returned to teach at Elphinstone Secondary School, to which non-Indian students were transported by bus from as far away as Sechelt. Within a few years, some Indian students who wished to continue their schooling beyond the grade eight level integrated at Elphinstone.

At about this time, I was having difficulty finding a thesis topic that would satisfy the University of British Columbia. After a few unsuccessful attempts, I suggested as my project a study of Indian education in this province. This topic was accepted by the university.

As my investigations progressed, it became increasingly evident that I could not obtain all my material from printed sources. Many questions arose to which there were no answers in either books or documents. Visits to residential schools throughout the province helped to answer some questions, but still left blank spots in the total picture. Some of these gaps, it became evident, could be filled in only by the Indians themselves.

I decided, finally, to visit the native Sechelt village. I had by this time made the acquaintance of several families, and had taught boys and girls whose fathers had once competed with me in athletic contests. Thus I came to visit the homes of the August, Paull, Julian, Joe, Craigan, Jeffrey, Louie, Jackson, and other families.

As the elders talked about bygone days, they referred, by their aboriginal names, to places still dear to their memories. I discovered, to my surprise, that the Sechelt people had not always lived in the village that I had, since my childhood, known to be their home. Once, they said, when their people were much greater in number, they had made their homes throughout the reaches of Sechelt and Jervis Inlets, carrying on a complete way of life beside and on these waters.

Just as my thesis was completed, I felt compelled to try to learn more about the culture of these people. Initially then, this story was intended to comprise nothing more than an ethnic study of one linguistic sept of the Coast Salish people. This task alone seemed adequate to absorb free days and hours for some time to come.

My first visits to the village took me to the home of Dan and Ellen Paull. I had met Dan some years before when he was cutting pulpwood on a piece of reserve land. Dan was a hereditary carver. Thirty years before, he had carved three totem poles with Paul Weenah from the Owikeeno people of Rivers Inlet, which stood near the beach as symbols of the native Sechelt. Ellen was a renowned basketmaker. Both had spent their early years close to the old ways of life.

It was Dan Paull who first aroused my suspicion that there was something more to his mythology than mere storied creatures. But Dan's command of English was not up to the task of taking me into his mystical world, and Ellen seemed not to know much about it.

While I was at the Paull home, Ellen's sister, Janet Fitz-Louie, and Mary Jeffrey, their sister-in-law who lived next door, sometimes visited. Mary vied with Ellen at making baskets, and Janet

seemed to know shadowy things about spirit powers of the shamans of bygone days. A Paull daughter, Sarah, had married
Andrew Silvey of Egmont, forty miles upcoast from Sechelt. I
sought out Sarah and was made welcome in her home also.

One of my first Native students at Elphinstone Secondary had
been Shirley Julian, whose father I had known from our school
soccer days. Shirley willingly answered my questions and, through
her insight regarding her people's former days, made me realize
that I must continue the search. Shirley's close companion was
Iris Joe. Through Iris, I came to know her father Clarence.
Clarence Joe was the Sechelt Band Manager. During my visits,
Clarence often said I should talk with his father. Basil, he said,
knew much about things from days that once had been. But
throughout the 1950s, Basil was away constantly, alternating
between logging and skippering seine boats on distant fishing
grounds.

Then, at nearly eighty years of age, Basil retired. My first
meetings with this patriarch were not auspicious. When I spread
an outline map before him and asked for some of his aboriginal
place names, he countered in a less than friendly manner. "Why
do you want our names, White Man? You stole our land. You stole
our fish. You stole our timber. Now you want our names. What
do you want with our names?"

At this time I had been corresponding with Major J.S. Matthews, Vancouver City Archivist, about local historical subjects.
Almost a year after my first unsuccessful meeting with Basil,
Matthews sent me prints from photos of the Sechelt taken many
years before. Some had been taken at the June 1890 dedication
of Our Lady of the Rosary Church, built with funds raised by the
Native Indians. Others showed Sechelt adults of that time, all
long since deceased.

Basil Joe was strangely moved by these old photos, a set of
which I gave him. He saw portrayed in them persons who had
been his elders at the time of his boyhood. While still studying
these likenesses, he suddenly said, "Take me up the inlet!"

This episode occurred during the late winter. Such an expedition would have to wait for summer. Meanwhile, Basil said that
he wanted to tell me the story of his ancestral Sechelt. He must
ask permission to do so, he explained, from Dan, senior member
of the Paull family, and from Agnes John, widow of a descendant
from a line of Jervis Inlet chiefs. On my next visit, Basil said that
he had been authorized by these two remaining elders to tell me
of things that he would otherwise have been forbidden to divulge.

Jack Gooldrup, a local boatbuilder who had spent his early years in and around Pender Harbour, had already taken me on one trip to the head of Jervis Inlet. On the way, we had come across an aboriginal rock painting, and we wondered about its meaning.

Altogether, Basil and I made fifteen expeditions, most of them in the company of Jack Gooldrup. As we passed places known to him since his childhood, Basil gave names to bays, rocky points, streams, mountain peaks, and onetime homesites. He also pointed out natural phenomena related to ancestral myths, and the largest pictograph of this people's traditional homeland. While we were on a four-day voyage up Jervis, Dan Paull passed away. Agnes John died not long after.

During stops on our journeys and in my visits to his home, Basil told stories, myths, and legends he recalled from boyhood years. During the last 2½ years of his life, he gave me a total of about two hundred place names, about one thousand aboriginal words, and a considerable body of ancestral lore. Using this material, a local artist created a map, ornamented with aboriginal features, which showed for the first time the names that the Sechelt had given to places throughout their traditional homeland. I wrote what I believed at the time to represent all that I would ever know about the prehistoric people.

Meanwhile, Jack Gooldrup was continuing his search for rock paintings. I accompanied him on many of these quests, but he set out alone on many other occasions. I photographed what he found. Almost all of the twenty or so pictograph discoveries made in Jervis and Sechelt Inlets during the 1960s resulted from the tireless efforts of Jack Gooldrup.

Following the death of Basil Joe in 1964, I continued to visit the Sechelt Native village. Basil's son Clarence, who had taken part in the four-day trip up Jervis Inlet, patiently answered questions during my many intrusions into his home. Andy Johnson, Janet Fitz-Louie, Mary Jeffrey, Ellen Paull, Cecile August, Jennie Erickson and others also gave freely of their time. Reg Paull, who had been trained in esoteric lore during his youth, could now speak to me about the Sechelt, since he was now the eldest in hereditary line. He told me things about olden times that pushed what seemed to be mere facts into mystical realms.

There they formed striking resemblances, in either name or kind – or in both – to elements in the mythologies of cultures far distant from the aboriginal Sechelt territory. Reading books and articles on world mythologies added further similarities. I concluded that the Sechelt had not, throughout ages past, lived in isolation from other cultures. Beliefs as mystical as those anywhere else on Earth had also been held here in these apparently remote inlets.

Whether or not the Sechelt were unique in this similarity to beliefs from other ancient cultures cannot likely be determined now. The last generation to bridge the gap between the old and the new way of life is gone. Sechelt did not come under close scrutiny by anthropologists. Only Charles Hill-Tout, from the University of British Columbia, and Homer Barnett, from the University of Oregon, undertook studies of any significance here before the middle of this century. They were limited, also, to conversing with Native informants either in Chinook or through interpreters, and failed to discover the mysteries that had once pervaded the culture they were investigating.

There can be no question that these Native Indian informants knew of their people's world of mysticism and spirituality, for they had been born into it. One of them, who was questioned through an interpreter by Homer Barnett in 1935, was father to Basil Joe, who retained much of this mystical element until near thirty years later.

But even if this explanation were true, and if other peoples also knew about these forces that influenced the subconscious, one would think that, despite taboos, somehow or other *something* esoteric would have been divulged as a result of all the grillings to which Haida, Tsimshian, and Kwakiutl informants in particular have been subjected over the past century. Killer whales, thunderbirds, ravens and the like have emerged as "storied" beings; but they mean no more intrinsically than do wild boars, stags, and other creatures from Old World heraldry. Nothing has appeared from the lore of these other aboriginal peoples resembling NAHM, the cycle of life; TAH'-OO, spiritual distance in time; YEE'-OOK, the apple orchard guarded by serpents; HUHK-AHLS-SAY'-KO, the "Spring of the Gods"; the rings of stone built to SHEHL'-SHEHL, the Moon; TCHAIN'-KO depicted in the form of Caduceus of Hermes; a rock painting likeness of the Menorah; the ideoplasm-ego-super-ego concept, made manifest in a carved totem pole; or anything of the many other esoteric phenomena that infused the aboriginal life of the Sechelt.

Certainly many peoples other than the Sechelt seem to have acquired or evolved particular mythological quirks quite different from anything found among their neighbours but related to something apparently peculiar to another culture far away.

Almost every native ethnic group of North America echoes some inexplicable characteristic from an "older" culture. The puzzling factor regarding Sechelt lore is that there are so many mythological quirks.

Perhaps other searchers failed through the vagaries of time and language to penetrate the secrets of aboriginal mysticism. What I discovered at Sechelt led me gradually to believe that certain definite but delicately balanced criteria must be met for the oral transmission of mystical and spiritual lore to take place. Primarily, of course, the Native Indian informant must have learned his people's mythology in more than its superficial context. Then, he must have received permission from his aristocratic peers to narrate this lore. Even if these two conditions are met, the searcher will fail unless he can communicate readily with his informant. This involves both the practical considerations of language, and the more elusive matter of rapport. Even though I had known his son Clarence for some ten years, and had taught his granddaughter Iris, I gained rapport with Basil Joe a year after I had met him only through the chance discovery of photographs that took him back sixty years into the past.

Unless all criteria are satisfied, a searcher can miss important parts of the culture he is studying. Professor Hill-Tout's informants, Charlie Roberts and Frank Eugene, were too involved in their new Christian religion to speak of their aboriginal beliefs. Professor Barnett's spokesman, Joe LeDally, did not speak English. His son, Basil Joe, could talk of the natural world and could tell stories, legends, and myths; but he lacked the vocabulary in English to translate mystic words he had learned, during his boyhood, to recite in his ancestral tongue.

It was Reg Paull, who had been tutored by Basil, who explained the spiritual elements which had infused his people's culture in years gone by. Reg had received training in ancient and secret wisdom. A generation younger than Basil, he had also attended Saint Augustine Residential School, where he had learned music and had memorized masses and hymns in Latin. In relating symbolic and esoteric features inherent in his native lore, he moved easily from abstractions in the Sechelt language to equivalent abstractions in English, at times making use of an unabridged Webster's Dictionary to find the exact shade of meaning he wished to convey.

A departed culture is judged, generally, on the basis of its physical remains. Regardless of its mythology, a bygone civilization is said to have ranked high or low culturally according to the stone buildings, the metal artifacts, and the paintings that have survived from its time in history or pre-history.

The aboriginal Sechelt left comparatively few tangible relics. They did work stone for tools, they did work copper for personal adornment, and they did leave behind paintings at certain places along their shores. But they did not build stone on stone to form elaborate or enormous structures dedicated to gods and kings.

I sometimes thought of the human sacrifices and the cruel rituals that formed the core of certain civilizations high up on cultural scales; of slaves and serfs who had worked to raise fine buildings and who had laboured to maintain systems of belief and customs in which they had no part.

Then, listening to Basil Joe and Reg Paull tell of times gone by, I thought of the far more pleasant world of the Northwest Coast peoples. And I asked myself if their manners, beliefs, and customs did not indeed exemplify human culture as it existed everywhere before we come upon the highly stratified empires which now fill our history books.

If we wish to discover how humanity in its infancy looked upon its creation and the world into which it had been born, then we must look for a time and a place at which recognizable cultural groups still saw themselves as living in the same ways as they believed that their ancestors had lived when they had come into being, uncounted ages into the past.

Such peoples, maintaining a common core of mystical and spiritual beliefs, must have inhabited every continent of the globe at an age that has left only whispers of its existence for present-day searchers to try to comprehend. While military, cultural, and religious conquests were cutting links with the past throughout much of the world, Indians of North America continued to transmit from one generation to the next their accounts from a very ancient past. Free from massive intrusion by Europeans until a hundred years before, the Sechelt people maintained beyond the middle of the twentieth century vestiges of a protomythology; a knowledge of the relationship between the human race and its divine spirit. This book is an attempt to express something of that relationship.

Chapter One

HISTORY IS SPECULATION based on record. Record alone is not history. History emerges only when records have been subjected to the art of speculation.

Where, in time and space, is our story to begin? The Sechelt people have answers to both parts of this question.

With regard to the physical world, the Sechelt claim to have always lived along the shores of what are now called the Strait of Georgia, Sechelt Inlet and Jervis Inlet, on the southern coast of British Columbia.

Tom MacInnes, whose family brought him to this coast in 1874, made friends with Native Indians throughout much of Vancouver Island and the Lower Mainland. One of the numerous stories told him by these people was of a time long ago, when their ancestors lived in an age of great ease and golden weather and green abundance. Then Ice Giants came down from the sky and killed all the trees and nearly all the animals. MacInnes related the experience of these people in his legend of Ko and Klon, as told to him late in the nineteenth century:[1]

> Through years and years of desolation the sky was low and heavy overhead; whirling grey and then darker grey to all black. There were no colours in the sky. And it was that way for a hundred years, and then for a hundred years, and for longer than all these put together. Under the dismal roof, men no longer kept count

of time. How could they? For there was no change in the sky except that when it was not raining it was snowing, and when it was not grey it was black; and no time can be kept by that.[2]

Stories indeed were handed down by the few survivors to their fewer children; and among them the great story of one round, warm, yellow, moving light in the sky, and one cold but beautiful moving white light, changing its fashion of shape regularly from a horn to a ball and back again, and of lights that twinkled farther away on a shoreless lake of blue overhead; twinkling with many colours, and bearing tidings of seasons and changes in the affairs of men. But after a while and longer, this story was not given much credence by practical hunters, who had come alive to the reality of things as they were.

It was a tale for women and children and those feeble in age; although some birds were yet deluded with it, for they regularly flew away at a time after they were hatched; flew away in faith to find some truth of it...

But after what time no man can tell there came a day that was a real day. The sun broke at last through the thick entanglement of cloud; shining out of a pool of blue above, and sending its warm brightness down over the desolate world.

According to the stories told Tom MacInnes, Indians of British Columbia's northern inlets were themselves created by glacial action. Today, these people still point to grooves cut into steep granite shores and say, "The ice did that, long ago." Hearthstones and artifacts found below strata of glacial till near Massett, Queen Charlotte Islands, indicate habitation there during or before the last Ice Age – somewhere from 10,000 to 20,000 years ago.[3]

One of the most interesting and one of the most controversial of ancient legends concerns the Flood. This story, with slight variation, seems to be almost universal among peoples of the northern hemisphere who perpetuate their past through the oral recounting of it. Almost invariably, the story involves a mountain that plays a part in saving a tribe or nation from extinction during this cataclysm. But the prominence of this event in Biblical legend[4] has tended to cast doubts on all unrecorded Flood stories.

A classic example of a rebuff to this ancient legend runs something to this effect: A missionary travelled among peoples of the American Southwest, teaching stories of the Bible. A few years later, an anthropologist travelled among the same peoples, unaware that the missionary had worked among them. The anthropologist was fascinated to learn that they had a Flood story. When all facts became known, however, scholars inferred that the aboriginal Flood story had been learned from the missionary and simply repeated to the anthropologist. Since missionaries taught among all Native peoples before anthropologists reached them, aboriginal Flood stories have generally suffered from such inferences, that of the Sechelt among others.

Now, however free they may be with anecdotal stories, Native peoples do not readily impart their fundamental mythology. When they do, it is found, with the Sechelt at least, to be unacculturated with the mythologies of later arrivals. There is no well- known Sechelt story that deals with early contact between Indians and Europeans. No European words were grafted into the Sechelt language. Even a simple word like "pot" was ignored, and a Native term, HUNK-LAH'-LAH, devised to designate the common iron trade article. Contacts with European traders and introduction to Christianity did not merge into the storyteller's traditional repertoire, but took their places as separate facets in the people's way of life.

According to Sechelt mythology, tribal ancestors saved themselves from destruction during the Flood by mooring their canoes to a huge log jammed into the top of KULSE, or "Anchor Mountain," now known as Mount Victoria, at the head of Jervis Inlet. When questioned further about this most improbable tale, the teller explained that this story is merely the popular version of the event. Actually, he said, his people lived during the Flood epoch in a cave some distance up the slopes of MIN'-ATCH, the mountain immediately north of KULSE, and almost completely hidden from the inlet by the dominating Anchor Mountain.

The term "anchor" is thus an embellishment of a story that remains quite complete without the addition: The Sechelt people, to preserve themselves from the Flood, PAHT'-AHM-OHSS, sought refuge in a STAH'-PAHSS, a cave, on the slopes of a mountain which they designated MIN'-ATCH. Yet at some time they also contrived the apparently superfluous story of the anchor, which turns out not to be an anchor at all, but a log, to which their forebears supposedly moored their canoes at an altitude of 7,500 feet above the present sea level.

Perhaps in this instance the mythical log was simply substituted for the well-known anchor. But Native Indians rarely anchored their canoes. Light anchors were sometimes used on fishing trips; otherwise, canoes were invariably beached. Thus the term "anchor" is not even a logical substitute. The alternative must be sought within the realm of symbolism. From time immemorial, the ship and its anchor have symbolized preservation. The ancient Egyptian solar ship was designed to carry the human soul into eternity.[5] As the ship symbolized preservation of the soul after death of the body here on earth, so the anchor, a version of the Cross, the primordial Tree of Life, symbolized preservation of life itself.[6]

The mountain, far back in humanity's past, symbolized both a source of awesome power and a place of refuge. Ancient people quailed at the voice of the deity ensconced on one mountain, yet sought from another peak actual or symbolic solace from perils being encountered. The term "Anchor Mountain" can thus be interpreted as a synthesis of two symbolic terms, each of which represents preservation of human life. The search must be continued even further, though, if we are to discover why Mount Victoria was selected out of the area's hundreds of significant peaks, to be designated as the Sechelt's Anchor Mountain.

Again, an answer can be found in symbolic reference. Ancient Egyptians and other peoples in Central America adopted the pyramid for structures significant to life and death. To the Sechelt, the pyramid shape in stone symbolizes the human being, singly or collectively.

While Mount Victoria is not pyramid shaped, its beautifully tapered cone more closely resembles that figure than does any neighbouring peak. It is also closest to MIN'-ATCH, the cave mountain.[7] SLIAM-KAY'-AHM, Mount Wellington, whose thunder and lightning struck fear into the hearts of those lonely people, faced HUHN'-AH-TCHIN village from just a few miles to the south. KULSE, at their backs, lifted its peak of tranquility and preservation.

From Harrison Lake, through Squamish, Sechelt, Alert Bay, on up the coast and even into the interior[8] of the province, the Flood story with its Anchor Mountain varies hardly at all. The Kwahkwelth name for the mountain, KULS'-AHM, which the people of Alert Bay refer to as their "Anchor Mountain," is in fact almost identical to the Sechelt term.

The Sechelt name for the Flood, PAHT'-AHM-OHSS, is a term that can also be used to describe water running over the edge of a vessel. The phenomenon being described obviously involves water running, not water falling from the skies. Coincidentally, the word "potamus" is Greek for "river." A torrent of water of such proportions that it caused entire tribes to seek refuge on a mountain is a common source of legend in northern latitudes. What the phenomenon was we cannot know today. Perhaps it was related to the Ice Age run-off. Perhaps it had to do with the mysterious event when the world seemed to stand still. The Old Testament story[9] is only one of many accounts from peoples as far apart as the Chinese and the Mayans of this strange calamity.

Clarence Joe told of two closely related stories attributed by his ancestral people to PAHT'-AHM-OHSS, the cataclysm that was to become known as a "Flood" myth. In one, waters that rush out of Princess Louisa and surged across Jervis Inlet left a white whale stranded high up a mountainside. Years later, hunters came upon the skeleton of this creature. In the other traditional account, waters that pushed almost seven miles up the valley of TSOH'-NYE, the Deserted River, left a White Whale trapped in a small lake behind a barricade of rock.

The Sechelt make no pretense that remains of either creature could be discovered, Clarence stated. But they know from these ancestral stories that the whales were in evidence far back in time.

According to both oral and written tradition throughout much of the world, momentous cataclysms wracked its surface about 3,500 years ago. On this occasion, it was not a slow, silent accumulation of ice but a sudden ruction of the earth's rotation which brought about devastation to plant, animal and human life.[10] Until the middle of the twentieth century scientists tended to agree that the last Ice Age terminated approximately 25,000 years ago. Then, carbon datings of sediment in river deltas drastically reduced this figure. Examinations of sites as far removed as the Bear River of Alaska and the Rhone Glacier of the Alps produced results revealing continuation of glacial conditions until some time between 4,000 and 3,600 years ago. The accumulation of plants and animals from apparently widely separated areas into great commingled heaps, indicates transporting by some element much more sudden than the slow but pulverizing movement of an ice sheet. This global spasm, coinciding with the close of the Ice Age, overlay and altered much of what had been down by glaciers. Entire species such as the elephant, the lion, and mammoth, the mastodon, and others in North America were overwhelmed and destroyed.

It would seem, then, that the stories of Ice Giants told to Tom MacInnes and the stories told by Basil and Clarence Joe of whales stranded high above sea level in Jervis Inlet refer to separate and distinct phenomena. The first, although it endured through centuries of time, was less devastating to life than the second. No stories of the ancient age of ice survive in Sechelt lore. But a memory of horses that swam about and walked ashore do remain, probably from a time prior to that phenomenon. And the event now referred to as the Flood does survive in stories passed down from eye- witnesses to the event, along with a realization that the catastrophe involved far vaster surges of water than could have resulted from rivers swollen by rain or melting snow. Sechelt legends do exist, asserting the existence of Native Indians here prior to and during the last glacial period. While they have gone unrecorded, the very classification "legend" denotes a basis of some real phenomenon.

Artifact proof of life at any specific time in the past in a particular locality is not easily found. Stone objects tend to gravitate down through loose materials or humus soil. It is not possible, therefore, to state with certainty that an artifact found at a certain depth under the surface has lain at that depth for as long as some carbon-bearing object that can be dated. Since stone itself can be dated only from its origin, and not from the time it was fashioned into an artifact, determination of the age depends on the presence of some residue of wood or bone lying close by in the stratum.

But artifacts have been found, particularly around Egmont, as deep as eight feet under barren gravel, too far removed from any present-day stream to have been deposited by conditions that prevail today. Gravel is a material through which objects would hardly sink so far. The two phenomena which could account for the depth of the deposits are the Ice Age and the cataclysm know as the Flood.

Obviously, some artifacts that may have existed prior to the last period of glaciation would not have survived. They would have been destroyed or pushed out into coastal waters by the tremendous tongues of ice that pushed down river valleys. Perhaps on shores of protected bays little or no erosion took place. Objects may have lain in such places comparatively undisturbed until melting of the ice sheet covered them with layers of water-borne silt.

Since, however, pieces found at locations other than recognized homesites may have been transported there either slowly by moving ice or instantly by cataclysmic action rather than having been buried where they were last used, only the objects themselves and not the possible significance of their positions can be considered.

The question of how many human beings have occupied the area from west Howe Sound to west Jervis Inlet has not been and quite possibly never will be answered with any degree of accuracy. Such evidence as does exist points to an occupancy of many thousands of years.

Until the year 1960, scientists would credit no time more distant than 3,000 years ago to mark the appearance of aboriginal Indians at the Pacific Coast. Even this figure, proposed by Charles Hill-Tout following his investigations in 1907 of the then newly discovered Marpole Midden,[11] was regarded by many archaeologists as too large. Further excavations at the site were carried on during the 1950s under the direction of Charles Borden of the Department of Archaeology at the University of British Columbia. These excavations confirmed Hill-Tout's estimates. Borden later discovered signs of human habitation 9,000 years old in the Fraser Canyon, not far above the town of Yale.[12] Stone tools found embedded in hardpan on the banks of West Howe Sound show remarkable similarities to artifacts found in Europe from about 20,000 years ago.[13]

There is no questioning the early occupancy of the Americas in general. Remains found as far south as Tierra del Fuego reveal the presence of human beings as far back as 15,000 years ago and as long as 100,000 to 125,000 years ago in California and Arizona.[14] Occupancy of the Northwest Coast is more uncertain. But if a disputed tenancy of 3,000 years can suddenly be rolled back to a confirmed 9,000, then the possibility certainly exists that the tenancy may be pushed even farther into the past.

One of the most puzzling and difficult questions in an examination of an archaeological site is whether the people who left the lowest stratum of artifacts were the same as those who left the last. Almost any excavation of an ancient homesite reveals some change in tools and weapons found at different depths. Obviously, either the same people remained at the spot and modified their appurtenances, or those original people were displaced by someone else.

On the basis on artifacts found at the deepest levels of lower Fraser Valley middens, scientists have deduced that the first peoples there were sea oriented, living on marine foods and fashioning implements and weapons from ivory and bone of marine creatures. Scientists also deduced that the level at which stone artifacts appeared in these middens marked the time at which Salish ancestors of present-day Indians invaded the area,[15] bringing stone technologies with them. It would be just as logical, however, to suppose that the original inhabitants may have gradually modified the medium and the style of their implements, through cultural borrowing and through adaptation to a changing environment during and following the Ice Age.

In the territory occupied by the Sechelt people, both bone and stone artifacts are found at all depths. Some individuals say that certain of these pieces were left by a people unknown to them. But this does not fit the claim that the Sechelt have always lived at the hereditary homesites. Possibly, the people largely forgot their ancestral stone technology, after abandoning their old tools and weapons.

Artifact finds do not, then, in any way deny the continued existence of the Sechelt Nation on the territory they account theirs since whatever time it was first occupied.

There is another type of evidence that tends to substantiate the Sechelt people's claim that they are not latecomers to their present locality, but have lived here from time immemorial. This is evidence in the form of deduction that can be drawn from Sechelt mythology. Here we must distinguish, as essential ingredients of the history of these people, such terms as "story," "legend" and "myth."

A story, among aboriginal people relates a memorable, but unembellished occurrence, which falls within the realm of possibility. The Sechelt people have many stories. From SWEN-AL'-NAHM, Moorsam Bluff, comes a favourite story about a mountain-goat hunter and his wife from the chief village of TSOH'-NYE, Deserted Bay. The hunter, so the story goes, had cornered a herd of goats on a vanishing ledge high up the bluff. Below, in their canoe, the wife began to compose a victory song to commemorate the anticipated success of the hunt. Suddenly, a young goat whirled about, leapt desperately back, and knocked the great hunter from the ledge. Watching her husband hurtling to his death, the red of his painted body against the gray of the granite rock, the woman changed her song to a lament and completed it. The song became a popular one among the TSOH'-NYE people, who added it to their paddling chants on their journeys up and down the inlets.

A story from HUHN'-AH-TCHIN features a young woman named KLAYA-KLAYA-KLYE – "Smiling All the Time." According to the story, the woman's husband and his two older brothers were hunting on the sides of MIN'-ATCH late in the year. Suddenly, some mountain goats they had been following disappeared. Upon searching carefully, the brothers discovered an opening in the rocks, entered, and found themselves with the goats in a cave. This was the very cave in which their ancestors had sought shelter from the Flood, long years before. A heavy fall of snow forced them to stay there during the winter. Then, one day, they were able to leave the cave and start back toward their village. When they caught sight of the head of the inlet far below them, they could see that their people, who would have spent the coldest part of the winter at SAUGH-KWAH'-MAIN, Pender Harbour, had returned to HUHN'- AH-TCHIN and were busy catching herring. As the brothers neared the village, they met some children playing.

"Is my wife home?" asked the eldest brother.

"No," replied one of the children. "She thought you dead and she has gone to live with another man at KUHL'-AH-KHAN."

The second brother received the same reply.

"And what of my wife, KLAYA-KLAYA-KLYE'? Is she home?" asked the youngest brother.

"Yes," said the children. "She still waits for you."

The story concludes that the HUHN'-AH-TCHIN chief then called a great KLUHN-UHN'-AHK, a celebration potlatch, to honour the faithful wife. People were invited from far and wide. A high swing, a KAY' KOH-TAII, its ropes of braided mountain-goat fleece, was erected. KLAYA-KLAYA-KLYE' was placed on the seat, but only chiefs could push her.

One of the few remaining stories of the former village of SLAY'-AH- THLUM, Brittain River, tells of a young man, SHOO'-LEE-UH, who was a great runner. This man loved a young woman at WHAH-WHOHT'-KWAHM, at the head of SMAIT, Hotham Sound. In the evening, SHOO'-LEE-UH would paddle to WHOHT-SAIL'-AIN, run through a pass inland to his sweet-heart's village, visit her, and return home by morning. Her people approved of the match; his, who were very proud, did not.

To atone for the slight to their pride, the young lady's people prepared a great quantity of gifts and foods, loaded them into canoes, and all paddled around to SLAY'-AH-THLUM. There they gave a TSOH'-LOH-MAT, a special form of potlatch held to show that a family is important, and not to be made fun of or insulted. In true dramatic fashion, the story ends here, allowing the listener to imagine whether or not the young couple lived happily ever after.

Stories such as these are assigned no dates. They could have occurred at any time prior to the disintegration of the old way of life that accompanied the intrusion of Europeans. As they are not identifiable with any specific event which can be dated, however, they cannot be used to peg habitation of the Sechelt people far back in time. Signs of such evidence must be looked for elsewhere.

Legends are founded on occurrences which begin as quite natural, although memorable and often tragic events; but which have gathered supernatural overtones. A typical legend is commemorated by a rock painting located between KWAY-KAY'-LAH and TCHEH-MUHM'MAIN, below Salmon Arm in Sechelt Inlet. The tragic event described certainly may well have actually happened. A man from SLAHLT, in the act of spearing a porpoise, was pulled overboard and drowned. But now some embroidery is added. For long after, the tale continues, people passing in their canoes would see the hunter in spirit form, sitting in a niche of the cliff above the scene of his death. They would call to him, but he would not come down. "I have been down to the Kingdom of the Porpoises," he would say. "I liked it there, and plan to return to it." This was no ordinary accident, but the work of TCHAIN'-KO, the Serpent—all powerful and the epitome of destructive force. To represent this, the head of a serpent, not the likeness of a porpoise, is portrayed on the cliff near the niche where the spirit sat.

A man from TCHAH-TCHEH-LAITH'- TEHN-AHM had died, so another legend runs, and was interred according to the manner of the times, above ground on SIHL'-LAY-EHK, the ancient burial island below KLAY'-KO, the Sechelt Rapids. Not long after he had been laid to rest, the people of the village saw a STAH'-LAH-SHAN, a killer whale, swim up to the island. The whale was the Indians' embodiment of visible and surface forms of evil. "Would you like to come hunting seals with me?" the whale asked the buried man's spirit. As the villagers watched, they saw two killer whales swimming away.

Legends, like stories, are ageless. All that can be said is that they took place "a long time ago."

Myths are explanations that have come down from some time in a people's primitive, imaginative past, to explain why certain phenomena appear as they do. They are never articles of faith, imposed on a people by a religious authority.[16] While many stories were merely village history, unknown beyond a small radius, myths were common to the entire nation; from KYE'-AHKS, Gower Point, on the east, to KOH'-KWEHN- EETS, Land Bay, on the west. The fundamental mythology would differ very little from one chief's village to another within the boundaries of areas in which marriages and other ceremonies brought villages together. It would vary more as these boundaries were crossed.

One phenomenon all peoples have found it necessary to explain is creation. Sechelt mythology does not explain the actual bringing into being of the earth. It explains, rather, how that portion of the earth known to these people came to be as it was when humanity appeared. It also explains the appearance of humanity itself. In the beginning, the Sechelt say, the Divine Spirit, KWAHT-AHM-SAHTH'-AHM, formless and timeless, sent down the HUHK-AHLS' to shape the world.[17] The term HUHK-AHLS' designates a rasping action. The world was made into its present form, the Sechelt believed, by the gods rasping the mountains into sharp peaks and scattering small particles of stone along the seashore to form beaches.[18] In Sechelt mythology, as in the Dead Sea Scrolls accounts, creation gods were not involved in the origin of the sea.[19]

On the shore of a small bay about a half mile below HUHN'-AH-TCHIN, a rock formation resembles a giant chair. The spot is known as TCHEHN-AH'-WAHSS-IHN, "Where God sat" when he had finished making the world. It would, indeed, be a beautiful place for a divine architect to rest and view the fruits of his labour. Like a green floor laid from one wall of mountains to another, the inlet stretches southward as far as the eye can see. Waterfalls hang like silver threads from either shore, and berries grow in abundance.

Thor Heyerdahl relates a story[20] in which the people of Tambo de Urcos built a gold bench to commemorate miracles wrought by the man-god, Viracochas. A statue of pure gold, representing Viracochas, was set on this gold bench. Both were taken as loot when the Spaniards captured the city of Cuzco.

On a little island off Smuggler's Cove, a neat depression in native granite is full almost to the brim with clear, cold water, in which an unusual sort of cress grows. This, to the Sechelt people, is HUHK-AHLS'- SAY-KO, "The Spring of the Gods." According to this myth, soon after they had completed their work on earth, the gods were holding a feast at this spot. They realized that they had no water; whereupon, the chief god struck the rock with his staff. A basin appeared in the rock, into which water flowed. During olden times, travellers always stopped their canoes at this spot to drink of the spring's cool water, which, they main-tained, possessed medicinal properties. Water from this bowl does not overflow; invisible source and exit keep the level con-stant, below the rim.

Generally speaking, Sechelt gods, like Greek gods, interested themselves very little in the affairs of humanity. One account from Narrows Arm, that of WHAIL-TAY-MOH'-TSAIN, consti-tutes a rare exception. A man, so the myth says, was leaping back and forth across a small bay. The gods were irritated by his capering and demanded that he stop. He continued to leap. Suddenly they stopped him, midway across the bay. He is still there, turned to stone, a little more than a mile above KO'-KAH, the Narrows.

Every channel, so Basil Joe said, had its HUHK-AHLS', its stone figure endowed with divine power to guard over the people of its shores. According to timeless myth, should any one of these rocks ever fall, the people over whom it had stood guard would be destroyed. Travelling near the mainland shore of LEAL'-KO-MAIN, Agamemnon Channel, Basil pointed out a granite boul-der, standing tall and erect like a natural menhir above a glacial scree. This, he said, was the HUHK-AHLS' of that passage. What is now known as Siwash Rock, he said, was the guardian of the peoples of Burrard Inlet. Years before, Chief August Jack Khaht-sahlano had pointed out SK-JUNK', now Dougal Bluff, at the western entrance to Howe Sound, as the guardian of the people of KYE-AH-TAH'-WAHN, now the village of Gibsons.[21]

The western entrance to the Mediterranean Sea was guarded by the Pillars of Hercules in ancient times. In Greek mythology, the cultural hero Hercules, who performed the twelve super-natural labours for the goddess Hera, was one of the Titans to occupy a role[22] very closely akin to that of the Sechelt's HUHK-AHLS', who performed prodigious labours among the coastal mountains of what is now southern British Columbia.

One fascinating aspect of lore from olden times is that its categories will not stay put. When scrutinized closely, story, legend and myth tend to telescope into one another.

The story of KLAYA-KLAYA-KLYE', for instance, while seem-ingly not an old tale, and while seemingly focused on the young woman, includes within it an account of the return to the cave.

The story of the mountain-goat hunter of SWEN-AL'-NAHM also appears quite plausible at face value. In this story a rare breed of man pitted his agility against almost sheer mountain-sides. The puzzling element in the story is that it remains almost the only incident in which a Sechelt hunter is defeated. It is not the more likely grizzly bear, or the sea lion, but the goat which destroys the mighty hunter.

Halfway around the globe, we find a possible answer to this anomalous situation. The Greek word for goat is "tragos," from which the English language derives its word "tragedy." According to the dictionary, the singers in dramatic performances in ancient Greece were dressed in goatskins. This implies that, in ages past, the goat was featured in the tragedy of the Achaean, as well as in Sechelt lore. Over wide areas of the earth, the goat is used as a symbol of disaster or tragedy.[23] Since the Moorsam Bluff incident fits this universal symbolism, it is unclear whether it is a story or a myth.

The story of SHOO'- LEE-UH suggests a counterpart of even greater antiquity. In ancient Egyptian mythology, Shu was the son of Ra, god of solar light. Like other Pacific Northwest peoples, the Sechelt did not use the "r" sound. Considering this fact, and that "Ra" is sometimes spelled "Re,"[24] the difference between Shu'-Ra-Uh and SHOO'-LEE-UH becomes quite minor. Since the Egyptians did not distinguish between the "r" and the "l" symbol in the names of their deities,[25] the Sechelt pronunciation could well be that used in ancient times. In the languages of the Kwakiutls, upcoast neighbours to the Sechelt, the word "lah" means "sun." Considering also that SHOO'-LEE-UH left home in the evening, ran toward the west, and returned at dawn, he suggests the timeless Mediterranean myth of Apollo, whose celestial horses drew the sun across the sky each day.

Even myths, in the light of universal lore, tend to lose their individual characteristics. It is quite possible, for instance, that wise men of the ancient Sechelt Nation understood primary forces that altered, and continue to alter, the Earth's crust. Their association of mythological Raven and Mink with these forces differs little from universal concepts symbolized by the bull, the lamb, the lion, the eagle, and a host of other creatures.

The concept of an unusual spring created by divine power, its waters regarded as magical, is of course not peculiar to Sechelt mythology. Wonder at clear water welling from solid rock is universal to mankind. Drawing on the power of his god, Moses brought forth water from solid rock with his staff,[26] just as did the Sechelt's HUHK-AHLS'. Ancient Romans believed that the waters of a spring at the grove of Nemi, sacred to Diana and Egeria, contained magical and medicinal properties.[27]

Thor Heyerdahl, while studying mythologies of the Pacific,

learned that the Polynesians gave the name "The living waters of Kane" to a sacred spring said to be located in the far-off land from where their ancestors had come. Heyerdahl found one such spring surrounded by a ruined temple on Titicaca Island, located in the Andean lake by the same name.

Another of Heyerdahl's discoveries was that South Pacific islanders refer to a former homeland as "Hawaiki" or, variously, "Hawaii." The Hawaiian Islands, in turn, are said to have been discovered by a mythical "wandering chief" often referred to by a name meaning "The Straits of Hawaii," who came from a vast land known only as the "Lost Home of Kane."

Transposing the composite word "Hawaii" into an older form, Heyerdahl came up with "Hakai." He found Hakai Strait north of Vancouver Island, leading from the Bella Coola Valley to the Pacific Ocean.[28] The root name of the hero of the Nawitti Indians was Kane, who, they said, came to their people on northern Vancouver Island travelling on foot. Kane worked miracles, then married a "woman of the sea" and left them, going toward the west with her.[29]

Since the word "Kane" is found in the Sechelt language as well as around Hakai Strait and in Peru, the "Spring of the Gods" on its beautiful island of stone near Smuggler's Cove fits the description of the sacred spring referred to in Polynesian lore in as satisfactory a way as does any other.

Humanity came into existence, according to Sechelt mythology, when the Divine Spirit sent down to Earth certain divine but mortal anthropomorphic creatures. These beings were referred to as SPIHL'AHM-OHSS, which can be translated, rather loosely, by the phrase "First Man." The beings included both male and female, who founded the band of humans now known as the Sechelt. The SPHIL'- AHM-OHSS, then, were the divine ancestors of the Sechelt people. All Sechelt have a lineage reaching back to beings of divine origin. These beings were not gods, or spirits, but obviously were no common mortals.[30]

All living things on earth except humanity came from the water, say the Sechelt. Some creatures have remained in TSAIN'KO, the ocean. Some came to shore, but returned to the sea.[31] Others came up on the land and remained. Only the human being came down from the heavens.

Two Sechelt accounts specifically refer to creatures from the sea. One pertains to MOOSE'-MOOSE-SHAH'-LAH-KLAHSH, who the people of KLYE-AH-KWIHM, Narrows Arm, said would come ashore at night and wander about their village, always returning to the water before daylight. MOOSE'-MOOSE, they said, was a sea cow–but not, it would appear, the more familiar manatee.[32] The Spanish National Archives contain an old manuscript that tells of a sea serpent being swept up on the beaches of Santa Maria del Mar, Oaxaca, Mexico, in 1648.... 'It was a dreadful monster that was tossed up on the beach by the waves,' reads the manuscript. 'The people of the village saw it at daybreak after a storm.... These people were terrified because they saw it move and flop about on the sand. But as the day passed, the motion became less.... It was 15 yaras (41 feet) in length and 6 feet in height lying on the sand. The body was covered with a reddish-brown pelt like that of a cow. It had two forefeet...'"

Her home has yet to be seen. It consists of a small-mouthed cave at the waterline, slightly less than a half mile above KO'- KAH, the Narrows. The story states that no one has ever reached the end of this cave.

The second account features TAH-KAY-WAH'-LAH-KLAHSH, the ending of whose name, as with MOOSE'-MOOSE, means that he came from the water. The presence of MOOSE'-MOOSE was known only by the sounds of her grazing about the village of KLYE'-AH-KWIHM. However, TAH-KAY-WAH'-LAH-KLAHSH can be seen quite clearly today. He is a beautiful white horse with a black saddleblanket, made of stone as if painted on the sheer granite wall above Chatterbox Falls, the Sechelt's KOH-KWAH-LAIN'-AHM.

The SPIHL'-AHM-OIISS brought gifts "from the sky." Presumably, as with the Titans, these were secrets from the gods. For example, in Sechelt Inlet at SLAHLT, chief village of the TAHW-AHN'-KWAH people, the SPIHL'-AHM-OHSS brought the art of canoe making. At SKUHLP, Saltery Bay, the "First Man" had skill in carving yew paddles. His descendants learned from him how to make beautiful paddles.

So it was for other spots which later became well-established village sites. At TSOH'-NYE, Deserted Bay, three SPIHL'-AHM-OHSS brothers brought the art of weapon making. One brought the bow and arrow; another, the spear; and another, the detachable-headed harpoon. HUHN'-AH-TCHIN, at the head of Jervis Inlet, was the chief summer village of the LAHK'-WIHL people from the Interior. Here, the SPIHL'-AHM-OHSS was put down with the knowledge of how to contrive and operate a fishtrap. At KLYE'-AH-KWIHM, Narrows Arm, the people were given knowledge of how to catch and cure herring; and at SAUGH-KWAH'-TEHN, at the head of Blind Bay, the art of cooking clams, a fine bed of which was to be found at nearby AY-UHL'-AH-KHAIN, was passed down to the people. At TAHK-WHOHT'-TSAIN, St. Vincent Bay, a woman SPIHL'-AHM-OHSS showed her mortal descendants how to make fire, and how to preserve it between clam shells for carrying it on journeys.

Each group shared its gift with others, until the entire nation had acquired all skills. But each village maintained a special pride in the particular skill that it had received directly from the Divine Spirit[33] through its SPIHL'-AHM-OHSS.

One cannot overgeneralize on the basis of these myths. This much, however, can be put forward. First, all myths, even those that refer to a time as long ago as creation, designate local geographic features—far distant localities have no place in Sechelt mythology. Second, these myths and legends are quite extensive in number, covering much of what is basic to metaphysics. Taken together, these two pieces of evidence do give some substantiation to the theory that the Sechelt Nation has always lived in the territory that it now occupies. Artifacts found at all depths were probably made or received in trade by the Sechelt. One of the themes of this study is that cultural exchanges did indeed take place, but that fundamental Sechelt beliefs either originated in Sechelt territory or were borrowed not in recent times, but in distant ages.

Chapter Two

Descendants of these first divine but mortal beings found themselves in a world of strange forces. Chief among these forces were, inevitably, those that ranged themselves on opposing sides of good and evil. Deep beneath the ocean lurked TCHAIN'-KO, the Serpent, represented generally, but not always, with two heads. Sometimes there was one head at each end of his snakelike body. Sometimes there were double heads at one end. TCHAIN'-KO had the power to make himself invisible. Being blind, he could not see his victim. He was generally portrayed being guided by STAH'-LAH-SHAN, the Killer Whale.

Personifying good, and opposed to these two creatures of evil, were SKEMP'-KOOL, the Beaver, and TCHASS'-KHAIN, the Condor. The great White Whale, KWUHN'-AYSS—probably the sperm whale—also enters the picture as an adversary to SKEMP'-KOOL. The Beaver, wily with age, kept watch in all directions and built dams in streams to keep KWUHN'-AYSS out. The people of HO-HO-KWAH'-MAIN, at the head of Salmon Arm, could boast to other villages, "You have a Whale in your lake, but we do not have a Whale. The Beaver has built us a dam to keep the Whale out of our lake." The fact that the dam referred to was KLOH-HOHM', a great rim of rock over which water from the lake flowed, would indicate that SKEMP'-KOOL was no ordinary beaver, but like mythological Raven and Mink, of supernatural quality.

Despite the Beaver's care, the Whale did make its way into

some lakes. KWUHN'-AYSS, second lake up the Deserted Valley, gained its name, so the people of TSOH'-NYE said, from a White Whale who once lived in its waters. It could be seen, so hunters up the valley said, lying on the lake bottom during the day and, sometimes, rising to the surface at night to swim about, slapping its tail and blowing. The people believed that if the Whale were to leave the lake, it would go dry.[1]

Up above soared TCHASS'-KHAIN, the Condor,[2] protector and guide above the hunter. He had the power of two feathers, TCHIHM'-UHL-KHAIN–authority to do good. TCHASS'-KHAIN and his power were guarded by two wolves, WOHK-AH-NATCH'-AHM. The Condor possessed WOHK-AH-NATCH-AHM-NOUT'; that is, Wolf spirit power. Beneath his wings were the PAY'-TCHIM, the embodiment of bad little children who had been caught and burned by HAY'-STAHL, the Bogey-Man. Sparks from the burning children transformed into little birds–the Pine Siskin–and had flown beneath the wings of the Condor to seek refuge there.

Reg Paull, descended from a line of carvers, made a totem pole in the 1960s that was expressive of the entire Sechelt concept of good versus evil. Reg explained that this concept can be interpreted figuratively as well as literally. The Serpent, Whale, Beaver and Condor can be accepted as mythological creatures, each possessing its peculiar degree of good or evil. But they can also be interpreted as symbols representing degrees of good and evil inherent in the human being–the polarity of mind and matter.[3]

One is inclined, inevitably, to think that this symbolic reference to the ego and the ideoplasm, with the latter's libidinal characteristics, has been added since contact with modern European culture. But Reg Paull maintained this symbolism had always been in Sechelt mythology. In any case, this psychology, as the Sechelt symbolized it, coincided more closely with their way of life than many psychological schools of thought do with our complex present-day culture.[4]

Examined in this light, the Native Indian belief is not at all simple, but most intricate. Indian people raised in their own culture learned to peer into and comprehend clearly the inner drives that sometimes impel the human creature to commit harmful deeds. Understood as subjective forces, these forces were attributed to the blind, undirected will of TCHAIN'-KO, the Serpent–a complex symbol in all aboriginal mythologies.

The Sechelt people still retain stories of TCHAIN'-KO. Weapons could not stop TCHAIN'-KO, they say. TCHAIN'-KO could go through solid rock if he so wished. Any otherwise inexplicable pull or disturbance below the ocean's surface was attributed to the presence of TCHAIN'-KO. The Killer Whale, STAH'-LAH-SHAN, often found a target for the Serpent, human or otherwise, and guided him to it. Furious evil could then be vented on the object. In a recessed niche on the shore near KWAIT-OH'-SEE-AT, halfway between Princess Louisa Inlet and the head of Jervis, three Killer Whales are pictured, guiding TCHAIN'-KO to a target.

Even if the symbolism were to stop here, it would be complex enough. But there is more complexity still. For any emotion—even love itself—if uncontrolled can become destructive, and therefore an evil force. William Shakespeare indicates this possibility most clearly in his tragedy *Romeo and Juliet*. The opposing families endure each other's hate without harm. The tragic force in this story is not deep hatred, but undisciplined love.

We must be careful here to distinguish between sin, a transgression against a sacred law, and evil, an act harmful to the individual. As no stories seem to have come down of wrong-doing against the Divine Spirit, sin appears to have represented a negligible force in Sechelt belief; but evil seems to have constituted an ever-present threat.

One way to grasp the Sechelt's way of understanding the world, as opposed to modern Western philosophy, is to find an emotion present in one culture and absent in the other. Such an emotion is anger. Well known in Western cultures, it seems to have been entirely lacking in the way of life of the North Pacific Indian. While the typical Western reponse to injury or insult tends to be sought in physical or economic retribution—a demand for blood or money[5] from the putative wrongdoer—the aboriginal Indian sought satisfaction by means of the TSOH'-LOH-MAT ceremony. In this ceremony, the person wronged established his true greatness through giving to the perpetrator of the wrong more than he could give back. The family whose marriageable daughter SHOO'-LEE-UH's family would not accept descended upon SLAY'-AH-THLUM, not to demand, but to give.

Perhaps this recourse to the gentle retort can be explained by TCHASS'-KHAIN, the Condor—the symbol expressive of the power of good.[6] He is the mind; "the eye of the hand."[7] The mind, clearly, was expected to oppose, and to cause the hand to oppose, forces of evil. Reg Paull, as future hereditary chief, was steeped in the lore of his people while a young boy, by MAH'-TAH, his maternal grandmother. Her roots penetrated far back into the old Native way of life. MAH'-TAH emphasized that the Condor's power could dominate and defeat that of the Serpent. The super ego can, if it so desires, master the id; good is supreme over evil. When insulted, the human being cannot call on TCHAIN'-KO, the completely detached force of elemental power. He can, however, appeal to TCHASS'-KHAIN, his protector. He can repay a hurt, then, not with another hurt–for the Condor symbolizes only good–but only with an act of generosity: "If he demand of you your coat, give him your cloak also; if he ask you to go with him a mile, go with him twain."⁸

There is a Sechelt legend that illustrates indirectly the power in the force of good. Two hunters, very close companions, were seeking mountain goats on the steep slopes above SKUHLP. One hunter lowered the other down an impassable cliff to a rock ledge, below which the cliff fell sheer again to the ground far below. But the hunter holding the rope was actually very envious of his friend's prowess in hunting, although he had never before expressed this feeling. Overpowered now by a passion of envy, he dropped the rope and left for home.

Searching the ledge on which he was thus abandoned, the second hunter discovered a nest containing three baby condors. Patiently, he fashioned his rope into three small harnesses. When the young birds were able to fly, he fastened to each a harness, which was in turn attached to the remainder of his rope. By flying as strongly as they could, the young condors were able to slow the hunter's descent sufficiently to permit him to arrive safely at the base of the cliff.

In a typical Western tale, this would not be the end of the story. In the literature and mythology of ancient Greece, on which the ethical structure of modern Western cultures is largely based, a special deity, Nemesis, was contrived to avenge the wrong on behalf of the gods. Inspector Javert,⁹ one of the most compelling characters in nineteenth century literature, took his own life when he could no longer justify his pursuit of Jean Valjean, yet could not, by his code of ethics, refrain from his pursuit. The great interest in the story of the Count of Monte Cristo¹⁰ lies, not in the wrongly-imprisoned man's escape, but in his destruction of his vilifiers.

But to the Sechelt people the story of the three condors is quite complete. The power of these creatures was for good, not for evil. They could only help save the wronged man; they could not punish the wrongdoer.

The Serpent–blind and formless–was beyond reach of the will

either to begin or to cease action.[11] The Condor–"the eye of the hand"–represented the mind itself. So, wickedness did not dwell in the human mind, but originated in some obscure region beyond its ken. The mind could instigate only good, and could counter evil–uncontrolled elemental drive–only with good also. It could be presumed from the viewpoint of Western culture that such a philosophy, excusing the individual from physical blame as it seems to do, borders on fatalism. Perhaps it does. And perhaps Western culture has not tried very had to understand the complexities of so-called fatalism. For, among a people who live by this philosophy, while an individual who wrongs another of his kind may be absolved from blame on metaphyscial grounds, he is by no means exonerated socially.

In the aboriginal North American culture, social forces were powerful, and rank itself depended in large part on behaviour. In this culture, the commission of an untoward act, followed by the disgrace of receiving gifts from the affronted party, would have brought about an intolerable loss of face–another term with which European philosophers have failed to come to grips.

TCHASS'-KHAIN, the epitome of good, could counteract, but he could not destroy TCHAIN'-KO. Evil would go on, just as good would go on. KWAHT-KAY'-AHM, the Thunderbird, or Thundergod, could destroy STAH'-LAH-SHAN, the Killer Whale, but even he could not destroy the Serpent. For these people saw evil, not as a force in itself, but as a attribute of the primal life force.[12] This force must be harnessed, not destroyed. To destroy it would be to destroy life itself.

But the concept is complicated even further. TCHAIN'-KO, as god of the ageless sea–which predated even the HUHK-AHLS', the gods of creation–could give life as well as destroy it.[13] When depicted with a single head, as he appears below Nine-Mile Point, he symbolizes a force destructive to life. When portrayed twined and with the two heads face each other as in the Caduceus, the symbol of the medical profession today, TCHAIN'-KO denotes a force protective of life.[14] Yet any portrayal, as will be discussed further in another part of this story, can symbolize fertility–the very origin of life. No symbol portrays only evil incarnate, as does a representation of the Devil in the Christian belief.

TCHAIN'-KO and STAH'-LAH-SHAN were not the only manifestations of destructive forces. The SKOHK'-EEN, lesser harmful spirits, pervaded to environment. In addition, certain localities were bad or fearful. The sharp bare peak of SLIAM-KAY'-AHM, rising directly before the village of HUHN'-AH-TCHIN, crackled with lightning and thunder before a storm. SHAK'-KWOHT, a small cave on the shore of LEAL'-KO-MAIN, Agamemnon Channel was poisonous, so the Sechelt believed. It also attracted the first lightning of a storm.

Deep in the mythology of the North Pacific Coast appear the Transformers or Tricksters. These figures, in whatever form they took, came not long after the world was created. While they apparently took no part in creation itself, they altered some features of the world, distorted things and turned them upside down. In some localities, they were best known as Transformers who left the world as human beings later found it, and even transformed lower forms of life into human shape.

To the Sechelt, these pranksters appeared as Mink, KYE'-AHKS, and as Raven, SKWEET-OOL'. Whenever, paddling along a shoreline, a group of paddlers came across an unusual formation – a twisted or tilted strata, a hole which seemed to have been formed by the native rock having been pulled open, or other disfigurement of nature – someone would say "Mink did that," or "That is the work of Raven."

Just below KOH'-KAH, the Narrows of Narrows Arm, a fir tree, extremely bent in a series of upwards and downwards turns, grows out from the rocky shore about ten feet above sea level. Already there when he was young, Basil Joe said in 1962, the tree is called KYE-AH-KAY-WAHN'. It is named after mythological Mink, who twisted it out of its natural shape.

Up in LEG-OH'-MAIN,[15] Jervis Inlet, the granite shoreline at Patrick Point, KAL-PAY'-LAIN, looks as if pebbles were embedded in it. This effect gave rise to the myth SAY'-AYTH-KAHM; "Throwing a stone." Long ago, according to this account, boys used to throw stones across the inlet, which was quite narrow then, from TEHL-TUHLWAHN', a stream mouth just north of Deserted Bay. Then SKWEET-OOL', the Trickster Raven, one day kicked the sides of the inlet apart as they remain to this time. SKWEET-OOL', regarded by the Sechelt as male, also widened the mouth of Narrows Arm below the Narrows. The Sechelt point to where the imprint of Raven's feet appear on the rock of the southern shore just above SHARK'-AIN, Storm Bay. The marks of his wings appear on the upper shore directly opposite, at a spot they call POHL'-KLAYTH.

The creek mouth at Gower Point is called KYE'-AHKS in the Sechelt language; obviously through some reference to Mink, now lost to memory. About three-quarters of a mile above the Narrows in Narrows Arm on the left side, a distinctive rock about eight feet high stands clear of the steep shore like a rough statue. This is identified by the Sechelt people as KYE'-AHKS—Mink herself.[16] Nearby, a long pointed rock lying up the bank is Mink's canoe. Above it, still another rock represents Mink's boyfriend waiting for her. Here the likenesses in natural stone fulfill the essential function of mythology—they "bring the divine down to earth."[17]

Again, generalization as to the age of this mythology, or to the kind of people who would formulate it, cannot be pursued with any great certainty. It is quite likely that the identification of certain emotions and forces with particular creatures reaches far back into antiquity. The Serpent, Killer Whale, Beaver, Condor, Mink and Raven are but the most prominent creatures of a vast animism that saw life, or spirit force, in literally every element of nature.

Here again is an aspect of aboriginal life meagerly understood by people of cultures much farther removed from nature. Sophisticated interpreters of animism generally think and speak of it as a belief in which natural objects and elements were credited with living or spiritual force of their own.

Up-inlet from the niche on which TCHAIN'-KO the Serpent and STAH'-LAH-SHAN the Killer Whale are painted is a place known to the Sechelt as KWAIT-OH'-SEE-AT. The locality takes its name from a long, narrow opening in the rock there at the intertidal level. Although too narrow to admit a human being, the Sechelt say that this cleft is very deep.

Above the cleft, on a low cliff of darkened granite, a distinct human face appears in natural rock formation. Below it, a white collar encircles the neck and a white apron hangs down over the chest and abdomen. A dark stain on the rock gives the appearance of a pendant. Offshore from this spot, the Sechelt say that a White Whale, KWUHN'-AYSS, can be seen as a small white dot deep down in the clear water—surfacing from the depths, as Captain Ahab saw Moby Dick.

Nearby, a rock about six feet high, pointed at the top with three triangular sides sits on a rocky beach at a distance of ten or twelve feet from the base of a sheer cliff. According to Sechelt belief, this rock is moving slowly toward the cliff. When the rock reaches it, that moment will mark the end of the world.[18]

At WHAIL-TAY-MOH'-TSAIN in Narrows Arm, the boulder that depicts the man turned into stone by the gods is similarly in the shape of a rough tetrahedon pyramid. Now, as this boulder is identified as a man, so that which is near the head of Jervis

Inlet must also represent a man. It is not an inanimate object moving up the beach, but a human being–symbol of all humanity–shuffling slowly but inevitably towards eternity.

Even to one schooled entirely in this lore, a granite boulder does not possess a moving force of its own. These two particular boulders are not merely granite rocks, but also symbols of humanity.[19] Symbolically, then, they possess the characteristics of human beings. The Native Indian did not attribute cognition to inanimate pieces of rock. Just as the Serpent and the Condor symbolized forces within the human being, impelling him toward evil or good, so these pyramid shaped boulders symbolized all of the animate forces of human life.[20]

No doubt names for geographical and natural features were added to gradually, as people became more thoroughly acquainted with their tremendous coastline. As most phenomena named consisted of mountains, rocky points, creek mouths, islands and beaches–quite permanent and unchanging features–there is no way of ascertaining now how long ago they were named. Sometimes, though quite rarely, names survive that were assigned to natural features that did show change. One such is KYE-AH-KAY-WAHN', the tree distorted by Mink that grows out of the shore below KO'-KAH. Even though it could be comparatively old, it is of wood, not stone; it is not ageless. It appears from objects such as this that the Sechelt may have been adding place names to their vocabulary until close contact with our Western culture began to break up the old way of life.

Through their mythology and on the basis of artifact discoveries, there does seem, then, to be a body of evidence suggestive of a theory that the Sechelt Nation has lived where it now lives since very far back into the past.

Chapter Three

Explorers, fur-traders, missionaries, and, later, anthropologists, were not long in discovering that the aborigines of the Pacific Northwest fell into reasonably recognizable large groupings, some of which contained further subgroupings.[1] Stretching across the entire territory at the north, and reaching as far south as the Chilcotin district through the Interior were the Athabascan, or Dene, who extended as far east as Hudson's Bay. Tahltans, Sikani, Babine, Carrier, and Chilcotins comprised subgroupings of this larger group.

Reaching inland to the headwaters of the Skeena and Nass Rivers lived the Tsimshians, and, below them, with their area cut into two pieces by the present homeland of the Bella Coolas, were the Kwakiutls, or Kwakwelth peoples.

The Queen Charlotte Islands were occupied by the Haidas, and the west coast of Vancouver Island by the Nootkas. In the southeast corner of the province, the Kootenais lived as far west as the Arrow Lakes, where they bordered on the Interior Salish, a people comprised of the Okanagan, the Shuswap, the Thompson, and the Lillooet. Occupying the southern coast of Vancouver Island and the mainland from Bute Inlet south into Washington State to the Columbia River were the people who came to be known as the Coast Salish.[2] Although not all subgroups have endured, traditional general areas are still occupied by Native peoples of their lines.

Numerous subgroupings of the Coast Salish people remain

quite distinguishable today. At Cowichan, Quathiaska, Sliammon, Squamish, North Vancouver, Musqueam and Sechelt, quite compact villages form population centers.

The Indians themselves never, apparently, used the term "Salish" or any other term to denote all those living within the territory mentioned. Nor are they particularly in favour of such designation today. There never was, they say, any centralization, either of place or authority within this territory. They do admit, though, that there is a certain degree of logic in such classifications. They agree, for instance, that these boundaries formed the limits within which they traditionally married, prior to the intrusion of Europeans. Marriage ties tended, apparently, to establish intervillage alliances; warfare among groups within this territory was thus uncommon. Boundaries within which the Sechelt people lived can be established, then, with a reasonable degree of accuracy.

Language is usually given as another determining factor in the designation of the area known as the traditional homeland of the Coast Salish. Linguists maintain that there are similarities in the languages spoken within the Coast Salish territory.[3] The Sechelt people maintain that their language is unlike any other. At one time, they say, their forefathers could converse with other peoples, not because their languages were alike, but because everybody knew many languages from frequent meetings with these other peoples from earliest childhood.

When such traditional intervillage visits ceased, they say, they could no longer understand the speech of even their relatives born of daughters who had married into villages beyond Sechelt boundaries. For a time, until English became a common language, coastal peoples resorted to Chinook. Some of the earliest European explorers found Chinook traders far from their home territory, exchanging articles among other peoples. Captain James Cook, for instance, on his visit to Nootka in 1778, encountered a small group of these Native traders there. Since these intermediaries could not necessarily convey the original names of all goods, and since they were usually things not made locally, articles often became known by whatever terms they were called by the Chinook traders.

Gradually, contact with goods and expressions of European origin added to the basic Chinook, until what had begun as a purely aboriginal language became a sort of patois: a trade jargon. Some terms, such as "Klah-hanie," meaning "out of doors" retained its Native derivation. Others, such as "la-gome stick," meaning "pitch-pine"; and "she-lik-um," "looking glass," betray their respective French and English intrusions.[4]

Commander Richard Mayne, who travelled with Coast and Interior Salish Indians much of the time during his four years in British Columbia between 1857 and 1861, perceived that differences did indeed exist among the local languages. Mayne concluded that learning the number of tongues he would need would be impossible, and resorted to Chinook with all Native persons he met.[5]

Explorers, traders, and missionaries all made use of this "lingua franca" of the Northwest. Missionaries taught Native peoples whom they had converted to Christianity to read and write in this language. Many Sechelt, during the last years that Chinook remained in use, could read and write social letters using a syllabic script taught by Father Jean-Marie LeJeune.[6] Ironically, with the disappearance of this practical trade language early in the twentieth century, and having little opportunity to learn to read or write English, they found themselves illiterate.

Working as they did with speech only, aboriginal Indians became much more adept at grasping and imitating voice intonations than people from cultures where written language is relied on. Sechelt Indians of middle age in 1962 maintained that their grandparents could manage to converse with as many as a dozen other dialects. The grandparents would speak in their own tongue, yet understand much of what was said in the others. They themselves would do well to carry on a conversation with a member of even one other band, they said, the days of long frequent visits between peoples having gone. No doubt there are more likenesses of language among these related groups than there are between any Salish language and one beyond its boundaries, but this is about as far as speculation can be logically carried.

The word KUHL'-AH-KHAN, "fort," appears quite frequently among Sechelt place names. Although the fort, generally in the form of a palisade surrounded by a dry moat, has long ago disappeared from the western slopes of SKWAH'-LAHWT, Thormanby Island, existence of such a structure is remembered to the present day. Another KUHL'-AH-KHAN, which once stood at the mouth of SUH'-AYTS, now Lausmann Creek, near the head of Jervis Inlet, is also recalled through such stories as that of KLAYA-KLAYA-KLYE'. It was built, so tradition has it, to prevent the LAHK'-WIHLS from the Pemberton-Lillooet country from spreading farther down the inlet.

Moorsam Bluff, which gave the appearance of a gigantic stone fort, was named KUHL'-AH-KHAN by the Sechelt. KAY'-KAH-LAH-KUHM, a low granite dome at Selma Park, retained its dry moat and its lookout tree for some years into the twentieth century. The name, so the Sechelt say, means "little fence." It was the site of a little palisade, as was the slightly varied KAY-KAH-LAH'-KEY-AHM, the rock point at Port Mellon. The graves atop this wooded rock are those of TCHEE-OO'-EE and SAHK'-OO, brothers to Basil Joe's grandmother, of the Squamish people.

The Sechelt were fortunate in being surrounded by either Coast Salish or Interior Salish peoples. Some of these related neighbours must have met strangers beyond their borders in combat; but to the Sechelt, such terms as KAYK'-AH-NAHM, their name for the Chilcotin, merely designated a shadowy sort of Bogey-Man.

Although the Sechelt have no reference to conflict with their Salish neighbours, they do have many references to raids from the north. Raiders came south both to capture slaves and to acquire loot. The raiders were renegades, not led by regular tribal leaders. They apparently originated among Native peoples who had come into contact with European liquor and European weapons early in the nineteenth century. Many young men found the combination too much for continued observance of traditional ways of life. Through either choice or banishment they left their homes, often to gravitate into "guerrilla" bands.

Sechelt lodges were filled with dried meats, smoked fish, prepared berries and fruits. Chests, WIHK'-AHM, were filled with regalia – masks, cloaks, drums, rattles, and other paraphernalia needed at ceremonies. These chests also contained furs, the medium of exchange in the newly introduced European economy. The appearance of liquor accelerated the degeneration of traditional social structures, and the advent of the musket gave renegade gangs overwhelming power on surprise raids. Reg Paull's people, the TAHW-AHN'-KWUH, living peacefully along the shores of Sechelt Inlet, suffered greatly in these raids. The story of the last of such raids is the one remembered best.

According to this story, WHEE'-PUHL-AH-WIT, great-aunt to Dan Paull and Basil Joe, and undoubtedly ancestral relative to much of the present Sechelt populace, lived at TCHAH-TCHEH-LAITH'-TEH-AHM. From here, long ages before, the villagers had seen the spirit of a recently buried man turn into a Killer Whale.

At the time of this last raid – carried out, so it was deduced, by a party from somewhere in the Nimpkish area – all the men were away from the village, hunting in the mountains that stood behind it. The raiders killed all of the women except WHEE'-PUHL-AH-WIT, whom they took with them.

The Sechelt responded quickly to this outrage. Partly, no doubt, because their numbers had been greatly reduced through epidemics by this time, they sought assistance from the peoples of Squamish and Nanaimo, two of their allies. Three SKY'-AKTH, war chiefs; LUHM'-AH, from Squamish; TCHEW-HAYL-AHM, from Nanaimo; and TSUH-KHAL', war chief of the Sechelt led the retaliatory expedition. The TSOH'-LOH-MAT ceremonial giving could not, of course, be applied where a wrong was inflicted by persons beyond the Coast Salish boundaries. In any case, premeditated killings could not be excused in this way.

Some of the warriors, it would seem from the story, were armed with trade muzzle-loading guns. Traditional weapons, which may also have been carried, were lances, TCHAY'-KOH-NATCH, with which the warriors stabbed without relinquishing their hold. The expedition triumphed over the offending raiders, and brought WHEE'-PUHL-AH-WIT back home.

No exact date can now be assigned this event; but pushing back into time two generations before the active years of Tony Baptiste, who died in 1926 and who was a grandson of TSUH-KHAL', would seem to locate it somewhere around 1840.

The Sechelt tell a story of another woman who was taken captive; this time to the area of Fort Simpson, north of Prince Rupert. She escaped, and made her way down the entire coast of what is now British Columbia to her home. The part of this story that seems to intrigue the teller most is that this woman managed to survive on the only berries available to her at that time of year; those of the MUHM-TSEYE', the red currant, a fruit with very little nourishment.

Many writers have made note of raids by northern peoples on their more southerly neighbours. The very fact that old stories mention the existence of small forts, which raiding parties could easily have avoided, would seem to indicate there having been some sort of game in the enactment of the raids of that time. They must have followed prescribed rules before the coming of liquor and guns changed them. These very old references to coastal "raids" simply do not mention indiscriminate slaughter. Sechelt say, in fact, that the result – and perhaps the intent – of these intertribal incursions was to mix coastal populations through the transportation of females from one people to another. In this process, they say, so-called raids occurred not only from north to south.

Pauline Johnson's "Ballad of Yaada" seems to bear out this contention. In this story, related to the famous Iroquois poet by Chief Capilano, a Squamish expedition "kidnapped" the young maiden and brought her to their home at the banks of the Capilano River. Her heart broke when warriors from her people, the Haida, returned her to her former home. Forever after, so the story goes, the river has expressed in its varied sounds the lamentations of Yaada.

Later raids, such as that in which WHEE'-PUHL-AH-WIT was captured, did involve the massacre of many persons. SKWALTH, a grassy flat east of the mouth of Cockburn Bay, Nelson Island, derives its name, the Sechelt say, from the fact that much blood was spilled there. A timbered, flat-topped, rocky knoll north of SAHL-LAL'-UHSS, a pass at the head of Bargain Habour, was forever cursed by a powerful medicine man because of the slaughter suffered there by his people at the hands of early nineteenth-century raiders.

Chapter Four

How people explain their existence and that of their environment is one of the two questions that naturally come to mind with regard to their history. The other concerns the manner in which they organize their social life. The first is concerned principally with what happened in the past; the second, with what happens in the present.

The village was the basic social unit that formed the core of social life in the Pacific Northwest. Among the Haida, Nootka, and other coastal peoples, the village, fixed and permanent, was a readily distinguishable feature. With the Sechelt, however, no simple distinction could always be made.

Weather and food sources created here a situation that caused considerable cyclic movement of the population. The heads of Jervis Inlet and of Narrows Arm and Salmon Arm, cutting through the massive Coastal Range, became colder than the Strait of Georgia shores during most winters, and Jervis often froze throughout its uppermost ten miles. In addition, while inlet heads were without shellfish, with very few exceptions, coastal bays contained all varieties in abundance. The inlets, on the other hand, had the largest and best salmon streams; and only up some of their high, broad valleys did certain prized roots and berries grow. Many families, therefore, migrated up-inlet in the spring and down-inlet in the fall, seeking out food at appropriate times and places.

Thus, a Sechelt village might be found at one site during the summer, and at another during the winter months. Captain George Vancouver, on his voyage of discovery from Birch Bay north during the summer of 1792, noticed lodges here and there which seemed to be in a state of dilapidation, and which he presumed to have been permanently abandoned. In other places, he noticed small groups of Natives living in rather makeshift plank hunts.[1] It was some time before he realized that the disarrayed lodges were winter quarters whose occupants had removed wall planking to construct rough summer shelter. Inhabitants of winter villages would have had regular, traditional sites on which they would establish their summer camps.

About eighty food-gathering places of the Sechelt people have been recalled by elders such as Dan Paull and Basil Joe. Names for many more places are now lost. How many people must have lived along this coastline to have made use of this many food-gathering spots? Captain Vancouver estimated a population of 5000 during his survey of the area.[2] Elderly Sechelt have said that their grandparents used to speak of a time when there was literally "one smoke" from Howe Sound to Jervis Inlet, so numerous were the lodge fires. It is known that five large lodges stood, one behind the other, at SAUGH-KWAH'-MAIN, Garden Bay, where only one family lived in 1962. Fish were sought as far away as HWAYT'-EYE, the southern tip of Lasqueti Island, inshore grounds being insufficient to supply the great demand for this food.

What the organization of these villages was like 500 years ago we can only guess. The earliest period of which we know in any detail is the middle of the nineteenth century.

By that time, five chief villages existed; SLAHLT, TSHOH'-NYE, HUHN'-AH-TCHIN, KAL-PAY'-LAIN, and KLAY'-AH-KWOHSS. The village of SLAHLT took in a large area; all of Sechelt Inlet, Narrows Arm, Salmon Arm, plus the Strait of Georgia coast almost to Howe Sound. The populace of this area referred to themselves as the TAHW-AHN'-KWUH people. TSOH'-NYE also took in a large area; namely, Jervis Inlet from the north end of Nelson Island to Princess Louisa Inlet. HUHN'-AH-TCHIN territory seems to have been limited to the very head of Queens Reach. KAL-PAY'-LAIN was the central village for Pender Harbour, the lower end of Jervis Inlet to Lang Bay, and Nelson Island. SKWAH'-LAHWT, with its chief village located at KLAY'-AH-KWOHSS, in what is now Buccaneer Bay, claimed Thormanby Island, Secret Cove, Halfmoon Bay, and Sargent Bay.

It is possible that more independent villages existed prior to that time; but, by 1860, the estimated population of the Sechelt Nation had been reduced to approximately 600,[3] mainly through the ravages of smallpox and tuberculosis. Many permanent as well as temporary sites became completely depopulated; KYE'-AHKS (Gower Point), HWAH-SAM' (Roberts Creek), TSAH'-KWOHM (Wilson Creek), KOH'-KWEHN-EETS (Lang Bay), SLAY'-AH-THLUM (Brittain River), and SKWAH'-KWEE-EHM (Vancouver Bay), to name but a few.

Two former small homesites located at the head of Porpoise Bay, the Sechelt's AUTH'-OH-LEECH, figured after their disappearance in a legendary canal. The people were purported to have tried digging this canal across the neck of land to TSAIN'-KO, the Strait of Georgia.

TCHAHW'AHWP, one site, stood where the Porpoise Bay Road now hits the beach. The other, TSOH'-LAITCH, two hundred yards away, was located at the site of the present Porpoise Bay wharf. Midway between these two places, the people built a dam to impound the waters of the small stream that enters the bay at this spot. The dam formed a narrow pond that reached about halfway across the isthmus. From its upper end, a TSAY-LAHW-AY-TUHN, forerunner of the European logger's skidroad, ran to the beach near the south end of the present Inlet Avenue, close to the old village of CHAT'-AH-LEECH.

When the canoe of a local or visiting chief or aristocrat landed at either end of this route, it became the duty of young men from the nearby garrison villages to help drag it along the skidroad, an action known as TUH-HAHW'-AH-KHAIN, saving the traveller a voyage of as much as eighty miles around the Sechelt Peninsula.

For some reason, a story came into being that the Sechelt, at some time during the nineteenth century, had begun to dig a canal across the half mile isthmus of near-sea-level sand and gravel. According to varying accounts, the diggers either stopped of their own accord or were halted by federal government officials upon the realization of the tidal differences at Porpoise Bay and the Strait of Georgia.

We know these villages existed, both from the stories handed down to the present-day Sechelt and from the many stone artifacts[4] which have been recovered from where they are said to have stood.

Although no detailed history of any village in particular can be pieced together today, a general picture of village life can be reconstructed from information that has been passed along from aboriginal times.

Joe LeDally, interviewed in 1935 by Homer Barnett[5] of the University of Oregon, indicated sites of the lodges that had stood, until late aboriginal times, at SAUGH-KWAH'-MAIN, Garden Bay. Each chief village, he said, had its lodges there, reserved for winter ceremonies.

Basil Joe, son of Joe LeDally, retained the names of the lodges that had belonged to TSOH'-NYE, a high-ranking village. The first lodge, which fronted the beach, so Basil said, was called KAY'-LAHWT. It was a storehouse for foods. Especially when the TSOH-NYE people were to play host to festival visitors from neighbouring nations, great quantities of fish, meat, clams, berries and other foods had to be dried and hung or stored there. The second lodge, AY'-TOH-TAHWT, was a dormitory for TSOH'-NYE people and for their related guests. Other Sechelt villages apparently maintained similar lodges at SAUGH-KWAH'-MAIN for their annual winter visits there.

One lodge, the KLUH-UHN'-AHK-AHWT, was shared by all. This great building was designed as a single huge room and was used only for spirit dances. Allocation of space, at least in the central festival lodge, was thus quite specialized among these people.

It would seem that the family has always formed the smallest social unit of Sechelt society. The single family unit seldom lived alone in traditional times, however, but occupied a compartment in a large communal lodge. The size of the lodge would depend on the size of the group, KAH'-TSAHW, that considered itself a family unit.

From information that has come down from Joe LeDally, who died in 1936 at the age of eighty-six, the traditional TSOH'-NYE lodge at SAUGH-KWAH'-MAIN, located beside the stream that drains Garden Bay Lake, was one hundred feet long. Although this size seems very large, some observed by early Europeans were even larger. Simon Fraser, for instance, noted that a lodge at Musqueam, the site of which became known later as the Marpole Midden, was one hundred and fifty feet by ninety;[6] and John Rogers Jewitt, during his captivity at Nootka early in the nineteenth century, saw a lodge occupied by an entire village.[7]

Some Native peoples built gable-roofed lodges; others, "shanty" roofs. The Sechelt seemed to favour the gable roof; but, according to Basil Joe, used both the gable and the lean-to styles. In the construction of a gable-roofed building, as erected by

Northwest Coast Indians, three posts – tree trunks, sometimes of enormous girth – were raised at each end, the highest between the two shorter ones. Logs – again, sometimes giants of the forest – were lifted and placed in notches atop these end posts. The log lying atop the two middle posts formed the lodge's ridgepole. The roof consisted of long planks, wedged from the sapring of standing cedar trees. They were laid like tiles to shed the rain, and they projected some distance beyond the outer beams. As a result, the walls stood considerably beyond what would be considered the roof plates in a modern Western home. Louvers in the roof at or near the ridge permitted smoke to escape. Below these louvers wooden trays were suspended to keep rain from falling on fires below.

Walls were made by placing overlapping planks horizontally between pairs of small vertical posts. These planks were bound together with withes of cedar root through holes drilled in the planking. In this type of architecture, the roof depended not on the walls but on the massive ceiling beams for support.

It is possible that ancient Mediterranean architecture once resembled the style of the Sechelt structures. When for, instance, the Greeks began to build their temples in stone, about 600 B.C., they repeated former wooden designs. Doric columns, sometimes cut from single blocks of stone, were made to simulate tree trunks.[8] And we read, in the Old Testament account of Solomon's Temple,[9] that its pillars were not of stone, but of wood. As Hiram was taking away the cedars of Lebanon, during this time, the large trees of ancient Greece were undoubtedly also disappearing.

As wood was no longer available, Mediterranean builders turned to stone for their important edifices. They retained the pillar, however – the replicated giant tree trunk – including even the flutings, which all Northwest Coast Native peoples also used for decorative purposes on their posts.

The Sechelt gable roof corresponded to the ancient Greek Attic style. Cut from comparatively small cedars, Sechelt roofboards were dished so that they could be used to convey water. The Mediterranean roof tile no doubt imitated in baked clay a form that had once been fashioned from wood there, too.

Both Sechelt lodge and ancient Mediterranean temple were decorated with heraldic and legendary figures – shadowy supernatural beings significant to times gone by.

Invariably, in a communal lodge of this sort, the head man and his immediate family occupied a large space at one end, with related families living in divided compartments along each side. Fires for cooking, heating, and illumination were located down the middle of the lodge. Platforms against the wall of each compartment, some three feet above ground level, served as beds. Food was stored in large cedarwood chests, the KLAH'-PATH, and also hung from the roof. Ceremonial clothing was kept into another type of chest, the WIHK'-AHM. The floor consisted of woven cedar-bark mats placed on the bare earth.

Inhabitants of a village would be divided socially into three castes: aristocrats, the KWAHT-KWAHT-AHM'; commoners, the KWAHSS-TWAYT'-AHSS; and slaves, the SKAY'-OHTS. Since slaves were almost always obtained through raids on peoples beyond the bounds of established alliances, and since the Sechelt were not, generally, the perpetrators of raids, a slave caste played little part in their society.

Commoner and aristocratic classes, while undoubtedly crystallized at their extremes, permitted a certain amount of vertical mobility at the rather hazy line that distinguished them. Social status depended, essentially, on behaviour and ability. Aristocrats led in hunting creatures of the sea and beasts of the forests. Aristocrats did artistic, heraldic carvings and paintings. Aristocrats preserved and perpetuated the nation's heritage through the STAH'-OO system, by which each boy of an noble family was obliged to memorize, word for word, stories told him by his elders. The term STAH'-OO designated both the authoritative knowledge – the ancient lore – and the belief in such wisdom. Only a boy with a naturally retentive memory could be trained successfully. Such a boy was called TSUHK'-HAHK; that is, "Good Memory." Basil Joe could become a storehouse of information from the past only because he was, from birth, a TSUHK'-HAHK.

If a boy – generally, only an aristocrat – succeeded in mastering the lore according to STAH'-OO, he became a TAH'-OO, a term meaning, roughly, "I have learned it." This word, as with many other Sechelt terms, parallels in sound a word used in another language far away. The ancient Greeks used the term "Tah-oo," or "Tau,"[10] as the nineteenth letter of their alphabet. From it, the letter "T" is derived. As we also used this sound in the word "taught," it would seem logical to believe that the Greeks used it in the way the Sechelt did; that is, to mean "I have been taught; I have learned." In ancestral times, the people of Sechelt Inlet, whose chief village was SLAHLT, called themselves TAHW-AHN'-KWUH. These people, so Reg Paull said, had TAH'-OO; they had learned something unknown to others – something esoteric.[11]

Reg commented further on this learning of sacred lore. If an aristocratic youth had learned and could recite what he had been taught, he could apply to himself the expression TOH'-TOH-LAH, to designate, literally, "I come from the STAH'-OO; I believe in STAH'-OO." TOH'-TOH-LAH could also be freely translated as "My place"; meaning that the speaker using the term felt that the TAHW-AHN'-KWUH homeland now "belonged" to him, in the sense that he knew about its past.

Aristocrats lived according to the highest moral and ethical code of culture. If a young man of noble birth were inclined to deviate from this behaviour, he might be admonished thus: "It is all right for the KWAHSS-TWAYT'-AHSS to behave in this way; but you must not—you are KWAHT-KWAHT-AHM." If a person born of noble rank stooped in behaviour, he ran the risk of falling in rank within his aristocratic caste, and even in caste itself. William Shakespeare, it may be recalled, has Prince Hamlet in his self-recrimination call himself a "rogue and peasant slave,"[12] not, obviously, because of any low rank, but because of his base behaviour.

In aboriginal times, tattoo marks, SLEECH, were used to indicate rank and heraldry. When the people were converted to Christianity, such markings were abandoned. Nevertheless, a certain amount of basic tattooing was retained. Basil Joe, although born years after the Sechelt had become Christian, recalled that his older sister had tattooed his age, during his boyhood, by a number of short parallel lines on his upper arm—one for each year—with a needle dipped into ashes from the lodge fire.

At the head of the nobility stood the chief, the HAY'-WOHSS. His status depended, to a degree at least, upon superiority in leadership. Heredity of title held good only providing the heir showed signs of competence; otherwise, succession might pass to some other member of the nobility, all of whom were of course related to the chief and to one another. Decision making was undertaken at meetings of all aristocratic adult males, much in the manner of the oligarchy of ancient Rome.

The man who acted as chief in normal times did not lead his people into battle. When fighting was to be undertaken, a special leader, a SKY'AKTH, was called upon. From what some of the Sechelt people say, we can infer that this individual led, throughout most of his life, a rather unusual existence. He dwelt apart from the village, with no fixed abode; and children were forbidden to go near him, lest he harm them. But, when an outrage against any of his people demanded retaliation, only he could lead the mission, as TSUH-KAHL' led the Sechelt warriors against the Nimpkish renegades to gain release of WHEE'-PUHL-AH-WIT in the story already related.

The presence of two leaders would attune with Sechelt philosophy. Just as the Condor, the symbolic force for good, could not combat the Serpent with evil, so the chief, who symbolized all that was best in life, could not lead in war, which, to the Sechelt, was no happy occasion. The HAY'-WOHSS could lead in situations where an affront could be settled by a gift-giving TSOH'-LOH-MAT. But only the SKY'-AKTH could lead if blood was to be let.

The kind of work done in a traditional village depended, not upon rank, but upon age and sex. Men hunted, fished, built, made tools and weapons and, when necessary, fought. Women cared for the children, made clothing, and gathered, cooked, and preserved foods. Children, from the time they were old enough to learn, received instruction toward adult life. Girls helped the women. Boys played games with miniature bows and arrows.

At the age of eight or so, gradual separation of the sexes began. A girl's training began to focus more specifically upon womanhood, and a boy's upon manhood. Girls swam in one place; boys, in another. At Pender Harbour, for instance, Garden Bay Lake was traditionally the girls' swimming preserve; and Lily Pad Lake was the boys'.

The boys made use of WAH-WAY-WE'-LATH, "Doesn't have sun until late in the afternoon," the cone now known as Mount Cecil, for their climbs, and for a part of their Guardian Spirit Quests. Atop it they built low groins of rock in the shape of serpents—representations of TCHAIN'-KO, the embodiment, in this instance, of fertility—fatherhood.

The girls climbed Mount Daniel, KWIHS'-TCHAHM, where, during puberty isolation, they constructed circles of small boulders, STUH-LAITCH', twenty feet or so in diameter. These rings indicated the influence of SHEHL'-SHEHL, the moon, with its lunar cycles.

Mrs. Mary Saul, raised in the Lillooet River country north of Harrison Lake, has said that, in her culture, a girl would spend nights during her time alone going slowly around her circle on her knees, reciting certain words as she reached each stone. She would take at least four hours to complete the circuit, Mary said. Her words were addressed to the moon.

With typical restraint from either worship or sacrifice, the

Sechelt resisted the creation of a moon-goddess, one of the oldest of deities. The puberty ritual, however, constituted the most sacrosanct of their ceremonies. Its symbol, essential to the ritual, was fashioned by the novitiate while she was alone atop her people's sacred mountain, preparing for their most revered state – motherhood.

While the names of the two lakes are lost, those of the mountains remain. Dan Paull never spoke of KWIHS'-TCHAHM, but with reverence. Its name could, so he said, be interpreted as "Hill of Gold." The crest of this mountain does turn golden in early spring, when myriads of yellow moss stamens come forth. The term "gold," however, has held a quite complex meaning in Western as well as in the Sechelt culture. In such an expression as "Golden Age," it could signify the highest point in cultural achievement, while in other usages it could be applied to an age of beautiful innocence.[14] The "Golden Mean" was a "Way of Wisdom," a philosophy of moderation. Jason's search for the Golden Fleece[15] involved the sacred, as did Saint Matthew's Golden Rule.[16] To Dan Paull, KWIHS'-TCHAHM was indeed a venerable mountain.

In addition to the part it played in puberty custom, KWIHS'-TCHAHM also served as a marriage site for inhabitants within the locality. This, according to Dan Paull, was for local, not intervillage marriages. In such a ceremony, known to the Sechelt as YAK'-SOHW-AHM, the couple were merely required to withdraw to the mountain, remain there for a time, and return, married, to their village. While atop the mountain they presumably exchanged vows, as long remained the custom at such spots as Getna Green, on the border between England and Scotland, without need of religious or civic official. The presence of the sound AHM in the name indicates, though, that there was a spiritual aspect to any Sechelt marriage.

Aboriginal peoples devoted much time to ritual bathing. Marriage was an occasion that required the intended bride and groom each to bathe in a specified pool or lake, in preparation. While the names of most of these once-significant places have been lost, the lake in which young women from SLAHLT bathed before marriage can still be identified. Known to the TAHW-AHN'-KWUH people as KOH-KOH-MAYTCH'-AHN, its outflow runs into Burnet Creek about a mile upstream from its mouth, a quarter mile east of the former chief village on the northern shore of Porpoise Bay.

A third use for the mountain KWIHS'-TCHAHM arose later

out of the raids from renegade bands from the north. When warning of such a raid came, women and children hurried up the steep side of the mountain to escape captivity. At the very top of the eastern peaks, overlooking what is now Madeira Park and Gunboat Pass, yet concealed from scrutiny from below, a hollow in the rock forty feet or so in length provided water. Mothers would know the spot from memory, for it was there that they had fashioned their moon-rings in the golden moss. Even when this pond seems dry in late summer, a thirsty climber can find water by digging into the sand.

Some time during the early 1900s, Fred Klein, pioneer of the locality now known as Kleindale, whose preemption occupied the site of bygone SMESH'-AH-LIHN village, climbed the mountain above his home to have a look at the surrounding terrain. There he found a series of circles outlined by flat granite boulders. These circles, some interlocking, still lie where they were placed untold years ago. Apart from rock paintings scattered throughout their territory, these rock rings, along with the S-shaped serpent symbols atop Mount Cecil, are the only visible remains of the Sechelt Nation to endure.

The adult division of labour among the Sechelt continued a separation of the sexes which began before puberty. Undoubtedly, this division served a purpose necessary to a man's ego, to a certain extent, in distinguishing which labour was manly and which was not. A man educated to this distinction learned to look upon fishing, for instance, as a manly and dignified enterprise, and upon berrypicking as unmanly and undignified. Yet fishing from a canoe at a creek mouth is not necessarily more arduous or more hazardous than berrypicking high up a mountainside.

Men's occupations often involved implements most like weapons, and often kept the men at the seashore nearest to where raids might be expected to come from. But probably the most significant effect of the division of labour was the almost complete separation of men and women during daytime. During autumn, however, all able-bodied individuals were usually up mountain valleys, the men hunting and the women gathering and preserving berries and roots. While the men hunted the deer, the mountain goat and, at the shore, the porpoise and the sea lion and seal, they were of course exposed to both the most violent exertions of strength and the most imminent presence of bodily harm.

It is difficult today to comprehend the power that lay in social forces within small, isolated groups of people. Shame was the one

unendurable feeling; weakness, the one unendurable characteristic. Not only could public disgrace cost a male his status
among other males; it could cost him his very manhood itself. It
a boy could not prove himself a man when the time came for him
to do so, he did not become a man but remained relegated to
unmanly labours. In the world today, a situation in which a man
works among women is considered not at all unusual. In aboriginal societies, however, a male would not do woman's work
with women unless forced to do so because he could not prove
himself a man; and in such a situation he would be considered,
by other men and women, as a woman.

Fear of disgrace or shame, SLAY'-UHL, also presented a powerful force to keep married couples together. Although a separation
also brought disgrace to the husband, the wife suffered the
severest humiliation if she was of noble birth. Leaving the mate
meant return to her native village, where she would be demoted
from the aristocracy.

Basil Joe commented on the process by which affairs were
conducted in a village such as TSOH'-NYE, in Deserted Bay, his
birthplace. The chief and his adult male aristocracy would sit in
a circle, so Basil recalled, to discuss matters on which decisions
must be made. Each member of the ring was entitled to offer an
opinion – carefully weighed, so that it would not bring discredit
to his reputation. He must, among other inhibiting conventions,
avoid telling a lie. What the Western world had long recognized
as a wrongdoing significant enough to make perjury a criminal
act, the Sechelt did not classify by a single and exclusive name.
They did use the expression KAY-KAY-WHAHN'-AHM, meaning "persons inside (of you) speaking in many voices" to indicate
what was considered to be happening when an individual uttered
a certain type of statement. The word STUH-LAITCH' was also
employed on such occasions, to imply that the speaker was
talking, as is sometimes said today, "in circles." A KWAHT-
KWAHT-AHM' too much inclined to STUH-LAITCH' would en-
danger his position within the aristocracy.

A member of the lower class could not participate in such a
policy discussion. Were he to seat himself among the noblemen
and attempt to speak, they would, so Basil said, "laugh and
laugh." Her persistence in trying to speak would merely bring
more laughter, until the luckless person would find himself even
lower down the scale within his own class.

Aristocratic women undoubtedly arrived at decisions regarding their group undertakings in the same manner as did the men,

although apparently not in so obvious a forum. The wife of a chief was distinguished by the generic term HAY-WOHSS-SLAH'-NYE. This highest-ranking aristocratic female would in all probability lead discussions on women's activities, in which she too would participate fully.

Chapter Five

Aboriginal Northwest coast peoples built no monuments or structures of standing stone. That they could work stone is made evident by their skillfully carved hammers, chisels, axes, and lance heads. Surrounded by lofty peaks, the Sechelt seemed to feel no need to add mankind's efforts to the works of the HUHK-AHLS'.

A people who not only looked up at their towering peaks from sea level, but who could also view their territories from high up these ranges, could hardly have failed to become deeply involved in their always-present mountains. The Sechelt's involvement with KULSE, which saved their distant ancestors from the Flood; and with KWIHS'-TCHAHM and WAH-WAY-WE'-LATH, sacred to motherhood and to fatherhood, respectively, have already been referred to.

Across the river known as SKWAH'-KAH from KULSE stands Mount Alfred, KUHL-KUHL-OHSS', at 8,500 feet the inlet's highest peak. To the Sechelt, it resembled a huge fort, and its name commemorated this likeness, just as Moorsam Bluff was called KUHL'-AH-KHAN because of likeness to a giant's palisade.

At the southern end of Moorsam Bluff, twin peaks rise above SWEN-AL-NAHM, a stream mouth that marks the entrance from Jervis Inlet to Vancouver Bay, SKWAH'-KWEE-AHM. On a clear day, from a point off the mouth of this bay, at about mid-inlet, a viewer can see in the outline of each of these two

43

peaks a face, gazing up into the sky. The Sechelt called this phenomenon KUHM'-KWAH. These were two brothers, so the story goes, whose likenesses are perpetuated in the mountain tops.

A dominant peak, TCHAH-TCHAH'-TAY-MOHSS, can be seen from near the mouths of both Salmon Arm and Narrows Arm. Another, MIH-TOHK', can be seen from their upper reaches. Neither of these prominences, one above Gustafson Bay and the other at the head of Misery Creek, is accorded a chart name.

To the north of Princess Louisa Inlet, SWAY-WE'-LAHT, the gloomy figure of TUHK-OHSS' broods. This term, said Reg Paull, could be roughly translated to mean "Old One-Eye." The expression "one-eye" was so complex in meaning to his people that it cannot be truly rendered into English. It is reminiscent of the Cyclops, mythological one-eyed giant of Sicily, and of the Norse god Odin, who sacrificed one eye for the privilege of drinking the waters of wisdom from the well of the wise giant Mimer.[1] Having learned the Sechelt story of this mountain, a traveller, from off Hamilton Island, can readily detect what seems to be a lone sunken eye beneath the crown of this distinctive peak, unnamed on present maps. TUHK-OHSS' is the physical embodiment in stone of a departed creator god, a HUHK-AHLS', standing vigil over this fascinating piece of water, from where PAHT'-AHM-OHSS, the Flood, burst forth long ago.

At the western entrance to Baker Bay, near the head of Hotham Sound, for which the Sechelt name was SMAIT, a sloping mountain resembling a man with his head thrown back in pride was so named KWAH'-TSAIN. Similarly, a hill about a mile towards the Rapids from Egmont Point received the name KWAHT-AHM'-OHSS, from the impression it gave of a "high hatter"; a dignified person.

SKWUH-UHL'-KHAIN, prominent peak inland from the head of Narrows Arm, reminded the Sechelt of the high middle lodge-post, notched to receive the great log that formed the ridge.

A peak, recorded on present-day charts as Mount Churchill, towers above SKWAH'-KWEE-AHM, Vancouver Bay, off Jervis Inlet. This landmark, visible also from as far up the inlet as the mouth of Princess Louisa, SWAY-WE'-LAHT, was called KWAY'-AHM-OHSS. It figures in one of the Sechelt's most compelling beliefs. If a climber, according to Reg Paull's explanation of this ancestral lore, were to climb to the very tip of KWAY'-AHM-OHSS, he would return "with the light in his face." He would have, as Reg put it, literally "seen the light"; he would have met a presence which affected him so deeply that he could not conceal it. It would have left an indelible mark upon his appearance. One cannot refrain from comparing this experience to that of Moses, who climbed Mount Sinai to converse with his god.[2]

Water falling down mountainsides and over rocks was TLOH'-KWOHM. Slate Creek, which appears on current charts as Stakawus Creek, was called TLOH'-KWOHM in bygone times because of its rocky course. Fresh water trickling down a rock, as occurs in many places throughout Jervis and Sechelt Inlets, was called TSAH'-TSAH-TLOH'-KWOHM. KLOH-HOHM', at the head of SKOO'-PAH, Salmon Arm, almost the only geographical feature to retain its aboriginal name, tumbles over a rim of rock into the turbines of the Clowhom hydro electric power station, and thence into the salt water. Down-inlet three miles, just below the "Bay of Owls," Misery Creek, fed by the snows of MIH-TOHK', hurls itself into the sea through a cleft in the rock. This jet of water, perpetually shrouded in mist, the Sechelt called WISH-IHM'-TCHIN, a term implying that the water is always cold. Over the mountains, HWYE'-OH-MAIN, literally "a crescendo of sound," forms a straight line for hundreds of feet through dark green forest before gathering into a beautiful pool, and thence into Narrows Arm.

From the sheltered harbours of the Harmony Islands, and from the landlocked waters of Princess Louisa Inlet, travellers pause for days at a time to be regenerated by the sight and sound of nearby waters. Between the south end of Granville Bay and Harmony Islands, the gentle thread of Freil Falls, TAY'-EH-KHAIN, drops down an almost sheer cliff seven hundred feet into Hotham Sound from Freil Lake. Nearby also is the massive bulk of KOH-KWAH-LAIN'-AHM, Chatterbox Falls. KOHTS-LAH'-KO, immediately up-inlet from Moorsam Bluff, plunges like water from a huge tap into its own mass of white foam at the base of its cliff.

There are many other waterfalls, especially during late spring and early summer. In June, the southern shores of Princess Louisa Inlet are lined with streams that plunge from ledge to ledge from the five-thousand-foot rim of mountains out of which this unusual chasm has been carved. A traveller passing along Queens Reach, the upper ten miles of Jervis Inlet, is never out of sight of a waterfall. Many of these perpetual white tumbling streams, fed by rain and snow, had names, but only the few mentioned here have survived of all the designations given to falling water throughout the Sechelt's homeland.

From almost any viewpoint, the Sechelt saw themselves surrounded by mountains. Some ranges were recognized as boundaries that separated their traditional homeland from that of the Squamish, the Lillooet, and the Klahuse people. Within these walls, the Sechelt built both physical and spiritual ways of life. They could see the mountain peaks and ranges of their neighbours on the North American continental mainland and on Vancouver Island. The wives of their nobility had been raised in the shadows of those natural piles of stone. Aristocratic children were descended as much from beyond as from within Sechelt territory. Yet the Sechelt language remained unique, and Sechelt myths, while similar in general to those of other Coast Salish peoples, were centered on local phenomena.

According to custom, each family was obliged to educate its young in ancestral mythology and legend. Successive generations would learn and transmit the lore that seemed to be as old as the rocks themselves. Children were told of the spirit powers that had created and transformed the "world" within their boundaries. As their families roved from one food source to another, the young were shown the natural features that were by age-old custom associated with these primal elements.

But an inherent urge that strove to maintain an ethos – a sense of spiritual, social, and moral identity – prompted leaders to do more than could be achieved by mere explanation. From a time as far back as tradition can be traced, the "spirit dance" and the "potlatch" formed twin keystones of aboriginal life. At the first ceremony, successive generations of adults, wearing appropriate masks and costumes, used chants and imitative movements to bring myth and legend to life. At the other, orators delved into distant times to trace the origins of the hereditary rights of certain members and families.

These ceremonies, repeated periodically throughout the ages, made a procession of younger generations aware of the relationship of humanity to the creatures of the sea, the animals of the land, the birds of the air, the mountains that surrounded the world, and the mystic spiritual forces that controlled and renewed life.

Chapter Six

Training of children took a quite different course in North America from that followed in Europe. One the hand, young Indian children were subjected to very little discipline; on the other, in seeming contrast, they were trained to endure extremes of cold, pain and isolation.

It was believed that freedom from restriction while a child was very young led to greater self-reliance at maturity. At the same time, boys and girls could see around them every day living proof that prestige in adult life depended upon learning very exactly the information and the skills the elder generation wished to teach them.

The environment, except for brief summer months, was a very harsh one, which made itself felt on all sides about the comparatively small village. One could not survive for very long removed from the stored foods gathered in co-operation with others. Perhaps this was felt by even the children, and caused them to be amenable to learning.

With boys, permissive discipline was employed during early years in order to secure courage later on. Courage in its ultimate sense did not mean rational adjustment to fear but a total absence of fear in the face of real danger. Absence of fear in adulthood can be attained only through its absence during childhood. So the Native peoples of the North American northwest coast raised their children in an atmosphere devoid of fear.

Behaviour was literally unrestricted during early, formative years. Free from punishment, the child grew to adolescence undistorted by a fear of parents, and free from fears he might transfer to other human beings and to wild creatures.

Seated on the beach at HUHN'-AH-TCHIN during a visit there, Clarence Joe would point over and over again to almost sheer cliffs along which his forefathers had hunted mountain goats, and say "You see, they were without fear!" They experienced, he would elaborate, no form of peril, from either another creature or from the possibility of falling from the precipitous cliff. To have been hampered by fear would have rendered their exploits impotent and at times would have led to extinction from lack of food.

While these people had no fear of the physical attributes of nature, they did fear what to them were supernatural phenomena. Such fear does not necessarily indicate inconsistency. Physical aspects of life were real, and produced results which, while sometimes fatal, could be measured and accounted for. Lightning, SPUHK'-AHM, and thunder, KWAHT-AH-MOHN'-ATCH, on the other hand, could not be accounted for logically, and could not be either predicted or measured. Perhaps, from far distant ages, the Sechelt people retained memories of storms that were indeed dreadful, and against which no ordinary degree of human courage could prevail.

So potent a part had storms played in their history that the Sechelt came to relate feelings of bravery and cowardice to this feature. Bravery, YAL'-NOH-WAHSS, meant, literally, "not afraid of the storm." TCHASS-KUHM'-ATCH, an expression indicative of fear and cowardice, was used to characterize a person who ran away from potential danger – particularly the dangers of lightning and thunder.

The Sechelt people did not seem to emphasize bravery to a point of physical mutilation, as some more warlike tribes in the continent's interior did. However, they did demand certain trials which would have proved too exacting for the weak of heart or limb, and which were certainly a more vigorous initiation into manhood than we demand today.

Some examples only of these trials remain. One took place about three miles below Patrick Point, KAL-PAY'-LAIN, in Jervis Inlet, on a smooth, steeply sloping black face of rock along the shoreline. The rock is slightly moist even in summertime over a distance of some seventy-five feet. Boys were expected to run across this surface, so slippery that it was termed YAY-KLAY'-NAHSS, the world KLAY'-NAHSS referring to oolachan oil in the Sechelt tongue. Failure meant a slide, on back or stomach, down twenty-five feet of bare rock into the water below.

About half a mile up-inlet from this spot, a point called KWAH-OH'-TAH by the Sechelt rises sixty feet or so from sea level. Boys aspiring to manhood were required to leap from this cliff. Even though the rock face is vertical, with an overhanging lip at its top, the clearance is not nearly that offered by a springboard. Paintings on the cliff face have also given it the name WY-AH'-HAH-LAHKS.

A few hundred yards above the lower end of SAUGH'-AH-NAH, now called Sakinaw, the only vertical cliff of the lake shore rises sheer from its waters. As story has it, a traditional trial of bravery required that a candidate for manhood swim underwater to this cliff from the shore opposite, a distance of about 200 yards. The task involved a test of courage as well as endurance. The test of bravery arose from a legend, according to which the lake was frequented by TCHAIN'-KO, the Serpent. The terrors that immersion in water inhabited by the Serpent must have presented to the Sechelt are almost incomprehensible today. Strangely enough, more than one European settler has reported the sighting of a monster near this very spot. One of the largest of all Sechelt rock painting galleries covers the cliff above the ledge at which successful candidates once completed their swim.

Another trial involving immersion took place at the foot of KOHTS-LAH'-KO, the waterfall immediately north of Moorsam Bluff, about a mile below Glacier Creek. Here, a very powerful jet of fresh water forces an amazing quantity of air beneath the inlet's surface. Candidates for manhood were obliged to remain underwater as long as possible, making use as best they could of the bubbles of air surrounding them. To surface before drowning was imminent would reveal unmanly fear.

Several oldtime Indians have related how, during their early years in a traditional lodge, they were sent out to swim first thing each morning, summer and winter alike, in order that they could endure water at any temperature. Basil Joe spoke often of his early boyhood spent in the lodge of his grandfather YIE-OH-MEET'-AHM. This lodge, which remained until almost the middle of the twentieth century, stood on the south bank of the TSOH'-NYE, the Deserted River, at its mouth. Every morning, so Basil said, YIE-OH-MEET'-AHM would send the young children, both boys and girls, down the beach to swim. Both boys and girls thus acquired an immunity against cold, and were trained to resist fatigue.

3 3600 00359 7950   BELLINGHAM PUBLIC LIBRARY
BELLINGHAM, WASHINGTON

Thomas Crosby, a pioneer coast missionary, commented on the endurance shown by Haida paddlers, who could cross the sixty stormy miles of Hecate Strait in six hours without rest.[1] Commander Mayne stated that, except for a pause ashore to eat, during which they did not attempt to sleep, men engaged to take him from Fort Langley to Fort Hope paddled all night. They would strike their paddles against the sides of the canoe with each stroke, and sing their Native songs all the while.[2]

The Sechelt people have many stories of hunters with so much agility and stamina that they could outmaneuver mountain goats along almost vertical bluffs.

Basil Joe, seated at the base of KULSE in his eightieth year, told of a time when he, his brothers, and the Johnson brothers had jogged to the mountain's 7,500-foot peak, after daring one another to do it. Passing by boat up and down his ancestral inlets – usually with Jack Gooldrup at the wheel – Basil would recite, as each peak came into view, how many times he had scaled it, sometimes, in a kind of joie de vivre, "just to look around." On bear-hunting trips inland from the coast in olden times, the traditional hunter took nothing but bow and arrow. More recently, he took nothing but his gun and some salt. Basil mentioned many times that once he had passed the timberline, he would strike out through the low alpine shrubs and flowers "and run, and run, and run."

Mrs. Ellen Paull recalled quite vividly the seasons during which she had carried each of her babies in turn up these same mountainsides in a basket, a POHT'-TSOHTH, slung horizontally across her back. Each day she would return to the beach at dusk, with both baby and berries.

Historians generally refer to the Coast Salish as having lived inactive lives. Actually, no European untrained in Indian ways could stand for very long the pace that the traditional Native maintained unceasingly. Steve Johnson, whose contempt of fatigue and cold became Jervis Inlet legend, gained his stamina through having lived and hunted with the Sechelt during his boyhood and early manhood. Steve was regarded with wonder by the hardiest of the non-Indian loggers and settlers of the inlet because he was almost unique in his ability to endure the Native way of life. Through much of his life Steve lived alone and homeless in the wilds of upper Jervis Inlet.

Training to endure or to disregard the phenomenon of pain also received much more attention from primitive peoples than it has from modern civilizations. Pain is, obviously, closely allied to both fear and extremes of temperature. Primitive peoples sought to control pain through detachment of self. Buddhist priests who burn themselves to death without flinching serve to remind the world that such complete disconnection of feeling from the body is possible. Aboriginal peoples seemed to possess this detachment to a degree almost unknown to Europe with the exception of a few martyrs. It is a feature, in fact, that perhaps best distinguishes East from West.

One of the paramount features of Graeco-Roman culture was the emergence of Self – the awareness in each human being of his individuality. While the West, particularly after the Renaissance, followed the path of emphasis on individual uniqueness, the East continued to emphasize the group.[3] When Europeans "discovered" America, they, in so doing, crossed the line that divided West from East.

The Northwest Coast Indians' detachment of self took the form of a submersion of the individual. Writers who began, during the mid-nineteenth century, to comment on ways of the Pacific Coast Indians, emphasized the degree to which a people working at a task requiring unison performed with complete precision and co-ordination. Commander Mayne noted, while travelling up the Fraser on the trips referred to already in this story, that his paddlers responded to sudden changes of the current as if they were a single entity, even during the blackest hours of night.[4]

The traditional Sechelt, like most other coastal aborigines, was virtually never alone. He hunted, fished, ate, slept, and travelled with his fellow villagers. Even when entirely alone, he had a companion, if he had danced at the sacred festival, his AY-YIHM'-UHSS. This companion was his spirit power, or Guardian Spirit – companion till death. Hunting large creatures of the sea or beasts of the land demanded for very survival on immersion of consciousness of self into the consciousness of the group. So deep and complete was this immersion that punishment for most serious crimes took the form of banishment from the village. Though alive in body, the banished individual was, to all intent and purpose, dead.

Immersed in the consciousness of his group, and within an animate, spiritual entity, the native North American lived a philosophy that found little likeness among European invaders. Each member of a community suffered, not as an individual but as an extension of his community, and without thought of time running out like the sands of an hourglass. Detachment of self, immersion of self in the group and in an eternity that did not pass gave to these people an immunization against fear, cold, and pain that is most rare in modern times.

Birth, to the people of the Sechelt Nation, represented an occasion of great significance, worthy of special rituals. A name handed down from a worthy ancestor was bestowed upon the newborn baby. In a sense, although perhaps not to a degree envisaged by the Hindus, granting the name of an ancestor to the baby literally reincarnated that ancestor.[5] Only names of illustrious forebears were drawn upon. The desire to have one's name, and with it, one's spirit, perpetuated, must itself have constituted a powerful inducement, in olden times, to live a good life.

A grandmother might sing a birth song, YAH-WIHN'-AHM, which the child would later learn, and a grandfather might tell as story about the ancestor whose name was being bestowed. The umbilical cord, carefully wrapped, was placed in a special birch or cherry bark container and hidden in a dry rock crevice as close as possible to where the birth had taken place. This ritual, called MAH-WHOY'-OH, gave the newborn a precise birthplace. Rather than the unenduring wooden lodge, a solid granite rock, the scene of the MAH-WHOY'-OH, became the conventional place of birth, giving a sense of permanence to this important occasion.

Heads of some aristocratic girls were subjected, soon after birth to binding with strips of cedar bark. Methods of binding varied throughout the Pacific Northwest. The KWIHS'-KOH-MOH, a term meaning "bound head," now known as the Quatsinos, made a continuous coil from the forehead back. The Sechelt placed a board, which was hinged behind, over the head, and applied pressure with turns of cedar bark. The board, slightly hollowed, finally produced the sort of tapered cranial structure considered appropriate for an aristocratic lady.

An individual, particularly if of noble birth, witnessed and participated in a series of ceremonies and rituals throughout life. Virtually all important ceremonies among the Sechelt took place during the fall and winter sacred season, when foods that had been gathered during the summer could be drawn on.

For about a month, from mid-August to mid-September, most Sechelt would make their way up mountain valleys to gather and dry foods. This annual excursion, known as a HUHL'-AHWT, ended with the appearance of the STUH-LAITCH'-SHEHL-SHEHL; what has come to be known in English as the "harvest moon"— the mellow full moon of September.

Upon its appearance, the people would travel to KLAY'-AH-

KWOHSS, Buccaneer Bay, on SKWAH'-LAHWT, Thormanby Island. There, they had built lodges[6] for each of the societies above its clean white sands. Just as in the European sense, a "lodge" implied both a building and those who met in it. Sea hunters, land hunters, craftsmen and other prescribed groups would each have their own lodges.

Each lodge was adorned with crests appropriate to the secret society to which it belonged. A central lodge adorned with all emblems – Raven, Bear, Wolf, Beaver, Eagle, Condor and others – housed the governing body of the societies.

In the water, on the beaches, and in the lodges, contests for competition and entertainment were held early each fall. These included canoe racing, running, drama, dancing, singing, and oratory. The occasion was known as a YEE-LAHL'-AHL-KWUH and was not, according to hereditary chief Reg Paull, a sacred event, but was mainly festive in atmosphere. Nevertheless, its patronage by secret societies must have made its functions quite similar to those held at Olympia.

One of the most significant of the Sechelt ceremonies was the winter dance festival. An individual qualified to take part in this ceremony was obliged to prepare himself for it long before the event. At some time between boyhood and manhood, the young aristocratic male set out on his HWUT-KWAHT'-TSOHT, a term that can be literally translated to mean "Guardian Spirit Quest." During the berry season, when he could sustain life in the wilds, he would leave his village to undertake this most significant mystic search. Usually, he remained on his own for several weeks.

Reg Paull explained this ceremony, much of which he himself had undertaken as a boy. Somewhere between the ages of ten and twelve, said Reg, the young candidate was required to go to a certain place. This was a spot between Brittain River, SLAY'-AH-THLUM, and HUH-AH-WAH'-MOHSS, a place at a stream mouth associated in Sechelt lore with a young woman weeping, up-inlet from SLAY'-AH-THLUM. About a half mile below HUH-AH-WAH'-MOHSS, a stream comes down the mountainside in a series of waterfalls. At a certain flat spot, the novitiate was obliged to rub himself with hemlock sprigs so vigorously that he drew blood, to cleanse himself in preparation for the spirit power dance. A candidate might be required to go to a certain chosen spot such as this for purification two or three years consecutively before he was considered ready for the spirit power dance. Hemlocks at the spot to which Reg Paull was sent were without tops and grew spread out from having been pulled by novitiates over the years, he said. Another spot to which a boy's elders might send him, and to which Reg said that he had himself gone, was located directly across Jervis Inlet from Vancouver Bay, SKWAH'-KWEE-AHM, in the vicinity of HOH-PAHL'-SHEEN, a steep windy ravine.

Leaping from the cliff at KWUH-OH'-TAH, running the slippery rock at YAY-KLAY'-NAHSS, swimming underwater across SAUGH'-AH-NAH, and remaining submerged under the aerated waters of KOHTS-LAH'-KO were some of the trials preliminary to the actual Guardian Spirit Quest.

The main element in the Quest itself came only after the candidate had proved himself brave and capable. After he had completed his trials and his ritual purifications, his family, as befitting their rank in the KWAHT-KWAHT-AHM', would stage a KLUHN-UHN'-AHK, a ceremonious occasion of feasting, oratory, and giving of wealth to make known the fact of the young man's manhood.

At some appropriate time after his KLUHN-UHN'-AHK, the young aristocrat would undergo his actual HWUT-KWAHT-TSOHT, the search for his Guardian Spirit. Their term KWUT-KWAHT'-TSOHT meant, so Reg Paull explained, "always waiting for anything; always alone; always looking for spirit power."

After days and weeks had passed, finally some sign would appear to the young searcher. Perhaps a tiny tree twig would seem to be giving off an unusual glow, forcing him to notice it.[7] Along with this visible sign,[8] a song would seem to come in the air, its words telling him the identity of his "Guardian Spirit," "second self," or "genius." The Guardian Spirit might be that of mythological, supernatural Wolf, Bear or Eagle.

Somehow, though, whatever other creatures may have been involved in the Guardian Spirit Quest, the Sechelt initiate seemed always to attain WOHK-AH-NATCH'-AHM-NOULT'; that is, "Wolf spirit power"—the spirit power of WOHK-AH-NATCH'-AHM, the Wolf. Although the Sechelt mythology says that the nation is descended from the SPIHL'-AH-OHSS, their divine ancestors; the Wolf plays a unique role in their genealogy.[9] A typical Sechelt "comic book" story might begin with an expression such as "Once upon a time,[10] when people were wolves..."
Throughout the Pacific Northwest, the Wolf, the Eagle, the Raven, the Bear and the Deer entered into the human lineage in much the same way that the Unicorn, the Boar, the Eagle, the Otter, the Stag and the Chamois once did in Europe. In fact, members

of this bestiary still appear in coats-of-arms and seals of such modern technological nations as Canada and the United States of America.

The Sechelt say that the wolf was never known to have harmed any of their ancestors. To the contrary, they tell of women who, returning to where they had left their babies hanging in POHT'-TSOHTHs at their berry picking camp, would find a wolf guarding them.

Wolf stories continue to a time even after the people began turning to Christianity. According to one account, a woman whose husband was too ill to travel left for a religious rally at Mission. While she was gone, neighbours observed a wolf carrying a bucket of fresh water to the invalid.

Just as certain aboriginal peoples of Burma and Indian felt and affinity to the tiger,[11] the Sechelt, so elderly persons have said, felt very close to the wolf. They never hunted this creature. Perhaps because its spirit had entered into the human being, they refrained from representation of this wolf in physical form among their carvings, except for the mask, which was meant to be worn.

Following his return to his people, the young man taking part in the quest dare not reveal the identity of his Guardian Spirit to anyone. He was watched over until the next YEE-LAH'-UHL-KWUH at KLAY'-AH-KWOHSS, Buccaneer Bay; or at SAUGH-KWAH'-MAIN, Garden Bay. There he would go to the PUHN'-AHW-TWUH, the ceremonial cave, where someone selected for this duty had maintained a fire since the candidate's departure on his Quest. He would dance to this person, with no others present;[12] and, as he danced, the older man beating time, KUH-WAH'-TIHM, he would gradually sing his SUH-WAHN'-OHSS, the song that had manifested itself to him in the wilderness, and that had revealed to him the identity of his AY-YIHM'-UHSS, his spirit power.[13]

Reg Paull emphasized that the spirit power dance had to be performed underground. If, as at Garden Bay, no natural PUHN'-AHWTWUH existed, the people constructed an artificial one by roofing over a swale in the rock and covering the timbers with boulders and earth.

The cave is a universally significant phenomenon, a comparatively rare natural hollow in the solid rock of earth. There is increasing evidence to support the belief that the popularly-known "caveman" age, an age during which almost all of humanity north of the Mediterranean lived in caves, in fact did not exist. It would seem that caves were used, even thousands of years ago, for sacred purposes and not as dwellings.[14]

It is believed that a chamber located deep under certain of the pyramids of both Egypt and Central America was a "Tank of Central Fire," as it is called in the Egyptian *Book of the Dead*. Just as ritual ceremonies performed in this chamber seem to have constituted only a portion of the many trials a novitiate would undergo during his investiture into the Sacred Mysteries in both Egyptian and Mayan cultures, the Sechelt Guardian Spirit Quest trial, with its isolation in the wilderness, its ritual song and its spirit power dance conducted in a chamber, also undoubtedly formed only a fragment of a vast mystic experience—perhaps an initiation into these selfsame Sacred Mysteries—only a vague shadow of which now remains with the Sechelt people.

The Essenes, before their sect was destroyed, entrusted their sacred scrolls to the sanctuary of a cave—a place that was to preserve them in safety for many centuries. The famous oracles of Greece made their predictions from within caves, the locations of at least some of which are still known today. India had maintained some of its hereditary caves. At appointed times, many thousands of pilgrims travel great distances, much of the way on foot, to participate in ceremonies perpetuated from antiquity at these venerated spots.

There is a psychological belief that the human being is born with a latent wish to return to the security of the womb, and that the cave intrigues humanity as a sort of substitute.

A cave other than the PUHN'-AHWTWUH was called a STAH'-PAHSS. The life cycle of the Sechelt was based on a series of visitations to the cave. At birth, the MAH-WHOY'-OH, the navel cord, was often left in the safekeeping of a dry cleft in the rock. Such a receptacle, a cherry-bark cup, beautifully styled and sewn and perfectly preserved, was found at Pender Habour in such a diminutive cave by June Cameron.

Basil Joe alluded to the fact that at least some of the aboriginal Sechelt males returned to their ancestral cave up on the slopes of MIN'-ATCH. In the telling of the KLAYA-KLAYA-KLYE' story, he implied that the three brothers had been searching not only for mountain goats, but also for the cave that had preserved their ancestors from the Flood. "My brothers and I—we found the cave once," Basil concluded.

At some time during the winter season, all young men who had acquired spirit power that year would be presented to an assemblage of the KWAHT-KWAHT-AHM', the aristocrats of the people, in the KLUHN-UHN-AHK-AHWT', the special "potlatch" lodge.[15] There, another aspect of the term HWUHT-KWAHT'-TSOHT manifested itself. The candidates were obliged by custom to make little of their encounters with the spirit world. A presentation assumed the form of an apology in the double sense of this word. From modest self-deprecation emerged an intimate glimpse of the profound mystic experience. The senior aristocrats, all of whom had undertaken the Guardian Spirit Quest, would recognize the duality implicated in such a presentation. The candidates were now admitted into all of the privileges and all of the responsibilities of noble adulthood.

The stages of progression to maturity undertaken by an aristocratic Sechelt youth could be classified under the proto-mythological headings "earth, air, fire, water." All four of these forces, recognized by mankind since the dawn of time, played a part in aboriginal Sechelt maturity tests.

From what has been gleaned of their purpose elsewhere, it seems most likely that these feats were used here, too, as steps in the search for something beyond self.[16] In the Guardian Spirit Quest, the novitiate was attempting to find a "second self."

The plunge from the cliff at KWUH-OH'-TAH, in which the diver would be forced far under water; the swim underwater across SAUGH'-AH-NAH; and, especially, the immersion beneath KOHTS-LAH'-KO, caused the participant to comprehend both the insignificance of self and, at the same time, the relationship between self and the entirety of life.[17]

Fire was used also in these aboriginal trials. It was used as a source of light in the PUHN'-AHWTWUH, the cave in which the AY-YIHM'-UHSS took place.[18] At other sacred places, such as the niche at KWAIT-OH'-SEE-AT, signs of old fires remain today. Even in the bright light of day, the novitiate was taken to an artificial source of light for his ceremonial initiations.[19]

We do not understand the precise details now of any of these manhood rituals: the swim under water, the exposure to wilderness, or the dance by firelight. But then, neither do we comprehend the full meaning of such parallel present-day rituals as baptism, the fast, or the altar candle—vestiges, perhaps, of ancient sacred rites much like those of the aboriginal Sechelt people.

The acquisition of guardian spirit power by females among the Sechelt was a quite unusual phenomenon; throughout most of the area within which this quest played a significant role, it remained mainly an attribute of the male sex.

The Sechelt did induct some aristocratic females as well as males, however. The name WHEE'-PUHL-AH-WIT signifies the fact that the young woman who was abducted from her village near the Sechelt Rapids had taken part in a spirit power dance, the term WHEE pertaining to WHEE'-OOKS, the black paint worn by the novitiate.

The participation of both sexes in traditional ceremonies gives an indication of the quite real egalitarianism that existed among the Sechelt. Another indication that feminine influence was significant can be adduced from the handing down of hereditary and traditional lore by female as we as male elders. Also, while inheritance of title was patrilineal, rights to property could be claimed through the mother's as well as through the father's side of the family. A woman might also attain the power of AY-YIHM'-UHSS, the healing or destructive spirit power possessed by the SEE-AY'-UHK, freely translated as "Medicine Man."

Chapter Seven

Among more northern peoples, the medicine man or shaman had the important task of leading and coaching a novitiate during his secret society dance, at which he helped him reveal in song what specific spirit power he had attained. Among the Sechelt, all of the nobility officiated, individually, at such ceremonies; and the duty of the SEE-AY'-UHK consisted primarily of applying his supernatural powers to healing.

The Sechelt, in fact, recognized four aspects to the human being: the soul, SKWUH-EYE'-EE; the spirit, AY-YIHM'-UHSS; the mind, SLY-AHK-HAY'-WAHN; and the body; SMAHK'-WAH. An affliction of an individual could, then, consist of an ailment in any one of these four aspects.

Another healer was the WHOY'-WHOY, who was also considered a magician. Since the term WHOY signified a dance or a dancer, it would seem that this personage performed in his regalia during ceremonial occasions, magically curing the afflicted in the process of his ritual dance.[1]

Visible physical wounds, broken bones, rheumatism, and other common maladies were treated by remedies known to virtually all of the adult population. Application of these cures required no specialized abilities.

More serious among injuries was the intrusion of some foreign object into the body. A fishbone lodged in the throat was a common ailment of this type, as fish formed a very substantial part of the diet. The chief generally undertook to enlist the services of a healer when such an accident occurred in a village. Since powerful specialized healers were rare, those individuals who possessed great healing powers sometimes practiced over a wide area.

Basil Joe told of a time when his father-in-law had witnessed the removal of such an object. A boy from TCH-WAHSS'-EHN, the Ocean Park area near Point Roberts, had a fishbone lodged securely in his throat near the larynx. He was taken to New Westminster, where a medical doctor offered to operate. Declining the offer, the boy's people returned him to his home, and called in a SEE-AY'-UHK renowned for his ability to deal with this type of affliction.

The boy, so the story goes, was stretched on the floor on his back. The healer, sitting crosslegged some distance away, took a mouthful of water and spat it toward the patient. He then asked him to feel his throat. "It feels as if there is nothing there," the boy commented. "Here!" said the SEE-AY'-UHK, reaching out his arm and opening his fist. In the palm of his hand, he held the fishbone, covered with blood.

Most serious of all to the Northwest aborigines was loss of the soul—the SKWUH-EYE'-EE; literally "My life." Preservation of the soul—within the body during life, and in the proper haven for souls, KWAHT-AHM-SWAY'-UH,[2] after death—was of paramount concern to the Sechelt, as it was to all ancient peoples. A person who lost his soul withered away and soon died. A soul, also known as the SKAHL-MAY-WHAHN'-AHN when it appeared in the form of the small white owl, could be lost in one of two ways: it might stray from the body, or it might be stolen from the body by force by a MY'-SEE-AY-UHK, a wicked medicine man.[3] In either case, a SEE-AY'-UHK who possessed special soul recovery power would be called upon to return the afflicted person's lost spiritual part.

While such occasions were obviously unscheduled, their random occurrence did form a significant ceremony among the Native peoples. Since the treatment was carried on in full view of all the villagers, it both tested the shaman's powers openly and served as a public performance. The last medicine man soul recovery was performed, apparently, somewhere in Sechelt Inlet during the summer season, at the time of the late Dan Paull's grand-uncle, who, Dan said, recalled it from the time of his youth. This situation would place the event at about 1840. Following the people's adoption of Christianity a generation later, all such aboriginal practices ended.

According to the story that has come down to the present, on this particular occasion the patient was lying on the floor of his lodge, to all intents and purposes already dead. The SEE-AY'-UHK, after a certain amount of ritual, opened his cupped hands to reveal to the watchers ranged all around a tiny white bird. "See!" he said to his audience. "Here is this man's lost soul. It must be returned to him!" Then he placed his hands against the patient's head, pressed, and withdrew the hands, empty. The "dead" man, having thus recovered his lost SKWUH-EYE'-EE, arose perfectly well.[4]

Typical North Americans today might feel that many stories of the shaman or medicine man, if true at all, could have pertained only to an age now long ago. That this is not necessarily true is revealed by an account brought from the Arctic by Ross Gibson, great-grandson of George Gibson, after whom the village of Gibson's Landing was named.

Ross, during much of his fifteen years with the Royal Canadian Mounted Police following World War II, lived among some of Canada's eastern Eskimos. Cutt off from civilization far to the south during long periods of time, Ross came to know and understand the ways of these people intimately.

One summer, a small party of scientists arrived at the site of an Eskimo encampment at Resolute Bay during one of Constable Gibson's stays there. These scientists proposed to make anthropometric recordings, in an attempt to determine whether or not the people there were related to other Eskimos farther west, in Canada and Siberia.

One elderly man, Alex, was seated in his hut when the scientists came to make their measurements. He sat obediently while calipers were placed across his skull at various points. Their work done at this site, the scientists moved on, with Constable Gibson accompanying them. About three days later, at an inland encampment, a runner overtook the group to say that the old man whom they had measured was very ill, and would die.

Upon their return to the first camp, they found the man precisely where they had left him. He had not moved, so members of his family said, from where he had sat for the scientists. He had taken neither food not drink. He thought that the calipers had taken his soul, so they said. He was resigned to die.

Constable Gibson, drawing on what he knew of Eskimo beliefs, sat down beside the doomed man, imitating his pose. He then had the scientists place the calipers on his head, here and there, as if measuring it. After the operation had been completed, he stood up, indicating to the seated Native that he had not, indeed, been robbed of his soul. At this, the old man arose, assured that his soul had not been removed after all, and apparently none the worse for his ordeal. Eskimos far removed from southern Canadian culture are as concerned today for their souls as Sechelt Indians were up to – and beyond – the days of Dan Paull's granduncle.

While Christian churches still lay emphasis on the human soul, today's inheritor of European tradition is unlikely to take the possibility of losing his soul as seriously as did the Innuit encountered not so long ago by Ross Gibson; nor is he able to explain or comprehend the magic involved in the cure of the stricken Sechelt villager from bygone days. Although he may recall stories of ghosts while walking past a graveyard alone at night, and experience uncomfortable feelings, he believes Biblical miracles only in a figurative sense of the word. And he employs such expressions as "The eyes are the windows on the soul," "For the good of the soul," or "Modern art has no soul" without wasting many thoughts about the existence of any fundamental significance behind the uses of this word.

As the Sechelt people were concerned about the loss of their souls during their lifetime, so were they concerned lest souls of the departed return to plague the living. Burial of the dead hence became an important and an exact ritual. A corpse was usually not removed through the regular lodge opening lest its soul retrace its path, as an unbodied force, to bring harm upon the inhabitants. Frequently, a plank was removed from a side wall and immediately replaced, so that the soul, should it wander, would be thwarted in its attempts to gain re-entry.

Burial places were changed also, to hinder return of souls that might stray from their rather vague limbo; their KWAHT-AHM-SWAY'-UH. Now a tree, now a cave, now an island might be employed as repository of the dead. All three of these different types of site were employed by the Sechelt. Early European travellers and settlers found graves on many islands, particularly on one in Porpoise Bay, known to the Indians as MAH-KWAH'-LAY and called Poise Island on charts. Some seventy coffins, once sheltered in a wide, low cave below HUHN'-AH-TCHIN, were looted years ago of both bones and boxes. Skeletons have been found in swampy ground and also under tiny roofs at Garden Bay, SAUGH-KWAH'-MAIN.

Manner of burial itself was also varied, apparently for the same purpose. Some bodies were interred in the earth, some were stored in caves, and some were hidden in rock crevices on islands. Some were stored in trees, though this was not common with the Sechelt, and some were placed in canoes raised on posts as on the west coast of Vancouver Island. The funeral service was known as the KUHM-SAH'-LAH-KWAH. This service was conducted by a professionally trained orator, a KOH-KOH-LAH'-KWAHL, whose main duty consisted of speaking on behalf of the dead individual.

How the human soul came to be so detachable, throughout the entire world at one time or another, is now lost in antiquity. Obviously, the phenomenon formed part of the greater concept of good and evil, in the aboriginal sense of these ideas.

The soul, SKWUH-EYE'-EE was distinguished from the mind, SLY-AHK-HAY'-WAHN, symbolized by TCHASS'-KHAIN, the Condor. In Sechelt mythology, the soul consisted, at least symbolically, of a small white bird, which inhabited the body, SMAHK'-WAH, during life, and which left it at death for KWAHT- AHM-SWAY'-UH, haven for such souls.

The soul was also distinguished by the Sechelt from spirit in the sense of spirit power. Whereas each individual possessed a soul, spirit power, AY-YIHM'-UHSS, had to be acquired. It was gained only by those aristocrats chosen to perform a spirit dance, the SAY-YOO'-IHN, through a special type of song, the STAY'-LIHM. The AY-YIHM'-UHSS was never general, but derived from and associated with some creature recognized from immemorial heraldic times, such as the Wolf, WOHK-AH-NATCH'-AHM, the Guardian Spirit power of which was called WOHK-AH-NATCH-AHM-NOULT'.

Sometimes the soul turned into SKAHL-MAY-WHAHN'-AHN, the Sechelt name for the owl when it represented the human soul. The SKAHL-MAY-WHAHN'-AHN, then, on occasion, spoke in the voice of the deceased. As late as 1927, the widow of a Sechelt man, Alexis, was paddling into a bay near the lower end of KLY'-EH-KWIHM, Narrows Arm, when she heard an owl say in her late husband's voice, "I am Alexis; this is my logging jack," and other phrases.

When Dan Paull, who died in 1962, was lying in his coffin in state, a member of his family stated that she had seen a white bird standing on his chest. By the time others looked it had disappeared. But the image was real enough to make her cry out at the time.

During the last winter of his life, late in 1963, Basil Joe more than once made reference to the fact that he had seen a small white owl near his home.

Legends from many parts of the world involve birds as the souls of human beings.[5] In the religious beliefs of the Papuans of Oceania, the "soul-bird" plays and important role.[6] Adam was created through the Elohim breathing "the breath of life into him," so that Adam became a "living soul."[7]

Sechelt stories based on the duality of body and soul differ quite markedly in two respects from most other peoples' tales. First, they are inclined to be rather brief, in contrast to the rambling and often weird episodes of, for instance, some of the peoples of the west coast of Vancouver Island. Traditional Sechelt myths and legends frequently seem, in fact, somewhat abrupt and lacking in conclusion, with the listener left to evolve the logical ending. More distinctive even than the length of these myths and legends is their tone. Whereas the mythology of most of the globe tends to be heavy, moralistic and tragic, that of the Sechelt is, in general, comparatively light and without moral judgment.

The Biblical legend in which Lot's wife is turned into a pillar of salt[8] for having disobeyed God's will, for example, was told to serve as a dire warning against such disobedience. The story of WHAIL-TAY-MOH'-TSAIN is almost identical, but is told in a lighthearted vein, as if the thought of the gods turning the man to stone strikes the teller as slightly amusing. That no mortal being could ever really have leapt back and forth across the bay at this spot tends to bear out the belief that this legend simply grew out of the position and configuration of a boulder at that location, with no moral admonition intended.

One of the stories popular with the ancient Greeks, an essentially land-oriented people, was that of Hero and Leander.[9] In keeping with almost all other Greek stories, this one ends tragically. After the conquering the Hellespont repeatedly, the brave Leander drowned in its icy currents. The faithful Hero then flung herself to the rocks below her window, where the body of her lover had washed ashore. This is most romantic – and yet its romance is overwhelmed by its tragic ending. The story of SHOO'-LEE-UH is quite similar to the Greek story, considering the Sechelt's water-oriented existence; but, in contrast, it presumes not a tragic but a happy ending.

Apart from souls that occasionally strayed or were stolen, the Sechelt did not generally think of spirits as detached beings. A term incorporated into the Chinook jargon, "Tamanawass," was used throughout much of the coast to designate a spirit that could exist apart from the human being. A "spirit" dance was common-

ly referred to among Nootka and Kwakiutl Indians as a "Tamanawass" dance.[11]

The Sechelt, however, used only the expression AY-YIHM'-
UHSS to designate spiritual power. This power could be achieved
by an individual only through a lengthy and exacting series of
trials and rituals. It was a personal power, and could not exist
apart from the individual who possessed it. It could be said that
a medicine man with an evil AY-YIHM'-UHSS was a bad medicine man, known to the Sechelt as a MY'-SEE-AY-UHK, and
that a medicine man with a good AY-YIHM'-UHSS was a good
medicine man, an EYE'-SEE-AY-UHK. The contrast in the two
ideas lay entirely in the prefixes "MY" and "EYE."[12]

The MY'-SEE-AY-UHK played a significant part in aboriginal
Sechelt life, posing a constant threat to the souls of individuals
about them. While no specific name has survived to the present
day, relics attributed to these grim sorcerers have been found in
this area. These artifacts consist of stones, generally granite but
occasionally hard sandstone, varying in size from little more than
two inches up to several inches in width and thickness. Each has
a hole through its center that was obviously drilled by man.

As guarded bits of information that can now be learned indicate, the MY'-SEE-AY-UHK kept these special attributes of his
art strung at intervals along a braided cedar-bark rope tied from
post to post in his lodge. Commanding the spirits inherent in each
of these stones, he could make them move back and forth along
the cord at will. If he wished not merely to steal a soul but to
destroy it as well, he would cause the soul to be lodged between
two of these suspended stones, and then bring them together by
command alone, crushing life from the captured soul. Since the
victim was permanently deprived of his soul, his SKWUH-EYE'-
EE, his vital inner self, he languished and soon died.[13]

The MY'-SEE-AY-UHK would have at his command the SKOHK'-
EEN, evil spirits attached solely to the services of this fearsome
person, to aid in his wickedness. The bad medicine man and his
evil spirits seemed to have triumphed little among the Sechelt,
however, for no particular stories about them have survived.

The last great EYE'-SEE-AY-UHK among the Sechelt Nation,
apparently, was KWIHL-SOH'-PAH, who lived before the people
adopted Christianity during the 1860s. Reminiscences of this
storied figure have come down to present-day Sechelt through his
son, YIE-OH-MEET'-AHM, and through the latter's niece, TLIE-
AH-HUHM'-AT, who was famous up into the 1930s both as a
basket weaver and as a herb healer. KWIHL-SOH'-PAH used his

own potent AY-YIHM'-UHSS to combat that of whatever MY'-SEE-AY-UHK may have threatened his people during his lifetime.

One of his tasks consisted of recovering pilfered souls before the evil medicine man could destroy them. In his lodge at SAUGH-KWAH'-MAIN, Garden Bay, so Basil Joe was told as a boy by his great-grandfather, KWIHL-SOH'-PAH kept chests filled with skins of animals and birds. By breathing upon one of these pelts with his spirit power, he could restore it to living form. A heron could be made to flap its wings, and to dive into a pool made to appear on the floor, sending drops of water flying. For a bit of fun, a mink pelt, breathed into life, was sent scampering to frighten TLIE-AH-HUHM'-AT and other young children playing in the lodge.

In like manner, while the TSOH'-NYE people were at their home village during the summer, KWIHL-SOH'-PAH once caused a fisherman and his canoe to be lifted from the bay, high into the air, so that his lines hung useless. Then, he returned all to their original positions. Perhaps we can attempt to explain this type of phenomenon by the same means we explain how Moses transformed Aaron's staff into a serpent.[14] In their own day, among the peoples who experienced them, the events needed no explanation, but were as real as any other sensory experiences.

The Sechelt were quite aware of the fact that the SEE-AY'-UHK had power of hypnosis, TCHEEN'-AYT, over the minds not only of birds, snakes and other creatures, but also over the minds of human beings.[15] Whether or not those under his spell were aware that their actions, or those of the magician, were subject to TCHEEN'-AYT is an issue still subject to debate. Such a term as "mass hypnosis" is too superficial and too facile to explain the very complex phenomena that may be encountered here.

Chapter Eight

Most elaborate of all Pacific Northwest ceremonies was that which became known by its Chinook jargon appellation, the potlatch. The Sechelt people recognized two distinct purposes for this ceremony. One purpose was to save face by a display of greatness in retaliation against an insult, or any other occasion when a family's position might be questioned. The second purpose was to show heraldry, rights, and wealth at the time of a birth, a death, or a marriage.

The first, the TSOH'-LOH-MAT, has already been referred to as a concluding feature in the story of SHOO'-LEE-UH. The second, the KLUHN-UHN'-AHK, was by far the most common reason for holding the ceremony. So important was this ritual that the large lodge in which it was held during the winter season was called the KLUHN-UHN'-AHK-AHWT'.

After 1912, Native Indians of British Columbia were prohibited by law from holding potlatches. The main reason presented by those instrumental in its prohibition was that the ceremony had degenerated into a wild, uncontrolled orgy. This accusation was often valid, but it was by no means always so. Pressure from Native peoples finally brought about an easing of the unenforceable law.

My grandfather, John Buol, took his family from Wisconsin to the north end of Vancouver Island in the year 1909. They spent that winter at Halfway River, Holberg Inlet, making acquaintance there with a small group of Quatsino Indians, remnants of what had once been a village. Of this small group, the family became closest friends with a woman they knew only as Lucy. One day, Lucy came to my grandmother, lamenting that her canoe had drifted away. My grandmother tried to console her, but she continued to mourn, saying that the canoe had been like a mate to her; that she felt its loss as she would that of her husband. Just then, my grandfather, who had set out in his rowboat earlier in the day, appeared with the lost canoe in tow.

Before long, Lucy's husband called, to say that he intended to hold a potlatch to express gratitude for the return of their important possession. My grandfather protested, saying that what he had done was a mere trifle, but the Indians insisted. And so John Buol and his family became honoured guests at a Quatsino potlatch. My grandfather received Lucy's husband's musket, which he kept in his possession throughout his life. The family received cloth goods and beaten silver ornaments. There was no disorder.

In 1917, my parents witnessed a much larger potlatch, held illegally at the Beaver Cannery in Rivers Inlet. A young child, the son of a chief, had almost drowned. Despite the fact that the child had not lost his life, the family felt obliged to hold a ceremony. Invited guests and spectators–Indians and whites– filled the cannery net loft for the colourful affair.

Time after time, the mother of the child on whose behalf the potlatch was being held passed among the crowd, dispensing handmade gold bracelets, lengths of new cloth, and handfuls of coins. Again, as my mother told me, years later, there was no sign of disorder.

White culture tended to regard the potlatch as a rather ludicrous giving spree, in which a Native Indian family compulsively gave away all of its worldly possessions. It was, in fact, the ceremony upon which almost the entire social and political structures of such peoples as the Sechelt were based.

These people, it must be borne in mind, did not write.[1] Such records as birth, death, and marriage certificates, bills of sale, contracts, deeds, and titles did not exist; neither did written laws and regulations. All such records, essential to the life of any community, were committed to memory among the Sechelt. At intervals, then, to prevent details of such records from being lost, and to establish records at time of birth, manhood, and marriage, it became necessary for each family of the KWAHT-KWAHT-AHM', the nobility, who possessed all property rights, to create some occasion at which the family's heraldry could be reasserted and its fishing, hunting, and ceremonial rights reaffirmed.

As can be seen, the system which had evolved by the time Europeans arrived was a type of feudalism, much like that which existed in Viking and Anglo-Saxon homelands at the time of the legendary Beowulf. Property comprised intangible as well as tangible goods. Tangible goods consisted of lodges, hunting and fishing equipment, regalia, and large canoes, which required crews of paddlers to operate.

Intangible goods included the right of an aristocrat to be invited to a ceremonial occasion and to hold such an event himself. It also included the rights to sing certain heraldic songs, dance certain ritual dances, tell certain ancestral stories, and to be accorded a certain position in the aristocratic hierarchy. Such rights served even more accurately than did tangible goods as criteria of special status.

Property, in the form of real estate, was not held by the Sechelt in the sense we think of this term today. While boundaries between these people and their neighbours and between sub-divisions of the nation itself were established quite closely for political purposes, economically there existed a certain amount of overlapping, both beyond and within the nation's limits. For instance, fishing grounds around Lasqueti Island, HWAYT'-EYE, were shared by all peoples bordering the upper Strait of Georgia.

At the head of Jervis Inlet, the LAHK'-WIHLS, ancestors of Pemberton Valley's Mount Currie Band, were entitled to catch and cure fish each summer to such an extent that HUHN'-AH-TCHIN became known as LAHK'-WIHL village. Good river valley berry patches were also shared. The TSOH'-NYE mountain-sides, according to Mrs. Ellen Paull, who journeyed there each season until after the time of World War I, were rich with berries, tubers and roots. KOHK-LOH'-MAIN, Mount Spencer, which rises from the valley behind SKWAH'-KWEE-AHM, Vancouver Bay, literally means "a great lot of good things put away." Undoubtedly, its lower slopes were made good use of during summer food-gathering seasons. Moorsam Bluff, KUHL'-AH-KHAN, was a favourite mountain-goat ground for hunters from all villages. In fact, it is one of the few places at which these animals, SWAYT'-LYE, appeared and still appear close to the shore.

Intangible rights, including the right to bear a certain name, wielded so much force within aboriginal societies that they determined, as they did in Europe under feudalism, what bits of physical property a man might possess. Distribution of both tangible and intangible goods resulted in and made possible an internal hierarchy of rank among the KWAHT-KWAHT-AHM' itself. As far as can be discovered now, no precise ranks within the nobility were created and given titles. Yet members of a village group, or of a gathering from many villages, would recognize rank quite exactly.

Both opportunity and obligation to lay claim to some precise stratum in the aristocracy occurred at the KLUHN-UHN'-AHK.

While great quantities of gifts may have been dispensed at this ceremony, gift-giving did not form its base, nor did it impoverish the giver unduly. Similarly in Western society, the most conspicuous aspect of a wedding reception is its conviviality, yet an observer from some other culture would be wrong to think that the occasion was a purely gala affair, without significant basis. Gift-giving was apparently carried out during aboriginal times on a much less lavish scale than that commented on by Europeans during the nineteenth century.

Reg Paull, trained during his boyhood in native Sechelt protocol, made a yellow-cedar paddle in 1962 and engraved on it a stylized KWAHT-KAY'-AHM, the Thundergod.[2] The anatomical parts shown on the blade were arranged according to enduring tradition in such a way that a viewer could not assemble them mentally to create an image of this supernatural being.[3] This, said Reg, was no implement intended for use, but a ceremonial paddle, a SKWAH'-KWEE-AHM. Each visiting aristocrat was obliged to carve a SKWAH'-KWEE-AHM for presentation to the head canoe, the KAHM'-AH-WAYTH, the personage holding the KLUHN-UHN'-AHK.

The recipient could retain and display his collection of paddles as evidence of the occasion,[4] and each contributor was at the same time obliged to produce an exacting work of art. During traditional times, the family staging the KLUHN-UHN'-AHK would have been called upon to feed the multitude, who came primed to "eat them up." Gifts were undoubtedly distributed, but these must of necessity have consisted of hand-skilled pieces of ornament and clothing, which could not possibly have been produced in excessive quantities or have left the giver poor through their loss. Since recipients of gifts were required by long-established custom to repay their host's generosity, the potlatch assumed the characteristics of a sort of renewal process – all old worldly goods were given away, and new goods were received.

The arrival of fur traders gave birth to forces which deformed the ceremony, and, in so doing, did much to break up the Native way of life. First, independent traders brought goods that inflated and finally destroyed the Indians' economy. Then the Hudson's Bay Company, in a effort of compete with the freebooters, built trading posts, each of which attracted several entire Native villages to its vicinity.

All of these aboriginal groups, accustomed to recognition of only one chief, tried vainly, through an accelerated spiral of the KLUHN-UHN'-AHK, to create some supreme authority. Each of the competing chiefs, possessing goods and wealth from the trading of furs to which he held rights, not only gave away but also ripped and burned trade blankets in great profligacy. Many even broke valuable "coppers," highest symbols of his heraldic wealth, in attempts to reattain, ironically, their tradition supremacy.

As many as two thousand Indians from many different peoples were gathered about the city of Victoria during the early 1860s, living a strange, unnatural existence, some permanently uprooted from their native villages.[5] Similarly, entire villages from many miles in either direction clustered about Fort Rupert, Fort McLaughlin, Fort Simpson, and other coastal trading posts, leaving behind them all of the heritage accumulated by their ancestors. However, no trading post was built within the home territory of the Sechelt. Furthermore, although the Hudson's Bay Company established a post at Nanaimo in 1852, the Sechelt were not tempted to remain there during spring and fall trading expeditions. Their decision to retain their roots prolonged myths, legends and remnants of tradition even through years when the people appeared doomed to extinction.

The last KLUHN-UHN'-AHK was held at SAUGH-KWAH'-MAIN, Garden Bay, at the wedding of the paternal grandparents of Basil Joe, who was born in 1882. As has been already intimated, this season of festivities, the sacred season, began when northern reaches of the inlets became covered with ice, SPEY'-OO, and snow, SKOH'-MYE. To the Sechelt, it was not a long season. It lasted from about the beginning of December until about the beginning of February—at which time runs of herring marked the start of food gathering.

Chapter Nine

Even during the winter months, fresh foods were sought to add to what had been preserved from the summer before. Cod, SAH'-HOH, and salmon, YOH'-MATCH, were caught; cod, around reefs near the shore, and salmon farther out in the gulf when there were not enough fish inshore. Large hooks of yew wood, AH'-WAYL, were used. They were sufficiently open for the head of the fish to enter and were baited on the inner barb, which caught below the jaw. The hooks were attached to nettle fiber, SAY'-EW-SAY-EW, or to kelp lines for halibut. Triple-flanged lures were also thrust to the bottom and allowed to rise slowly to the surface for cod.[1] The fish followed the revolving lure up to within range of the fisherman's spear.

In June of 1962, I accompanied Jack Gooldrup to the head of Jervis Inlet. There, off the site of the former LAHK'-WIHL village of HUHN'-AH-TCHIN, we set down trolling gear, with leaders attached to heavy main lines, each carrying a five-pound sinker. Something took several leaders, along with flashers, before the delicately set trolling gurdeys could let the line run.

Jack returned to the spot, just east of the mouth of the SKWAH'-KAH River, with a piano-wire line. Again something struck and, after a prodigious turmoil, snapped this very strong gear.

Late in August of that same summer, Jack and I arrived at this fascinating place on an expedition with Clarence Joe and his father, Basil, in search of aboriginal Sechelt lore. Early next morning, with Basil at the wheel of the *Little Arrow*, we trolled in a sort of figure eight around the inlet's head near the river mouth.

After we had cruised for about an hour, Jack asked Basil why he was avoiding a certain area – the spot at which Jack had lost so much trolling gear.

"Because that's where the Hunachin Monster, SAH'-HOH, lives," Basil replied.

Years ago at this spot, according to Sechelt legend, a giant codfish had devoured a young HUHN'-AH-TCHIN girl from a group swimming there. The monster has remained at this place since that time, Basil said.

Some biologists say that fish which never leave the sea seem not to die of natural causes; that they may continue to live indefinitely until destroyed by a predator or by some environmental catastrophe.[2]

Jack Gooldrup found direct evidence of an unusually powerful creature. Basil Joe would not troll across that piece of water. Well past the midpoint of the twentieth century, something lived where the Sechelt people maintained that SAH'-HOH made his home.

Another sea fish used by the Sechelt for food was the capline, a variety of smelt, traditionally called TCHIM-AH'-NEE and more recently known also as SKWEE'-BEE. This fish, which spawns on beaches some time in October, was caught by means of dip nets, to be either cooked and eaten fresh or rendered for oil.

The anchovy, TSAY-PAY' NAH, was also prized for its oil. It was caught in fine nets.

The Sechelt say they did not go to the Fraser to fish for the oolachan and had no name of their own for it. They did, however, have a term KLAY'-NAH, for its oil.

TOHL'-KWUHTZ, the octopus, could walk on the ground like a person, the Sechelt said. Basil Joe said that his grandfather had once seen an octopus walking overland from the head of Porpoise Bay to Trail Bay at Sechelt.

Ducks were also hunted during the winter to add fresh food to the diet. Several methods were used to take these birds. One was by means of the bow, SLUHK, and arrow, HYE-EYE'-TUHN. Heads of these arrows were made from two long slices of split deer bone for maximum penetration. The bow was held in a horizontal position with the palm of the bow hand facing upwards. Thumb and forefinger of one hand squeezed and pulled the arrow back; forefinger and middle finger of the other hand guided its release. A slight swale ahead of the notch was designed to aid the bowman's grip on the shaft.

When ducks and geese were overhead on migratory flights, efforts were made to lure them down. Elderly Sechelt ladies frequently maintained that boys and girls were trained to imitate their calls; and that, when flocks of these birds appeared, entire village populations would call th them to land. Where ducks flew through narrow gaps between trees and rocks, collapsible nets were sometimes set up attached to long poles, and the birds frightened into them. Such a net, called a SUH-WAHL'-TUHN, once stood on the neck of land occupied by the shallow circular lagoon at SAUGH-KWAH'-MAIN, Garden Bay, one of the waters that make up Pender Harbour.

If the birds sat on the water beyond reach of bow or net, still another method of stalking them was employed. Hunters would paddle among the huddled flocks at night with lighted fires on clay-lined platforms which protruded beyond the prows of the SKWUHK, the special hunting canoes. As the canoes cut through the flocks, birds were blinded by the firelight and picked from the water before their eyes could readjust to the dark.

TSTAY'-WHAYM, the willow grouse, and HOHM'-HOHM, the blue grouse, although undoubtedly hunted by the Sechelt, were never mentioned as significant food sources.

The bluejay, TSKASH'-KASH, and the crow, TSKAY'-KAHK, seem to have been given names imitative of the sounds of their voices. The hawk's name, TSTAYT-KAY-NASS', indicated that he struck his prey in the chest. The names TSAY'-OO-TSAY'-OO for the osprey and TSKWAHK'-WAH-LAY for the kingfisher were given to these birds because of their penetrating eyesight. None of these birds were hunted by the Sechelt so far as is known; nor were HAY'-UHK-AYK, the common owl, or KLAH'-KWAH-KHAN, the swan. The Sechelt name for this latter bird is vaguely reminiscent of the Gaelic word, Ealachan.

It is quite likely that, far back in aboriginal times, there were quite intricate taboos among the Sechelt against taking certain creatures for food or clothing. While, for instance, PUHK'-UHL, the Gold-Eye Duck, was given a place in mythology, the actual bird was hunted as a food source. And although Mink, KYE'-AHKS, figured prominently as a mythological Transformer, the common mink was sought for its pelt. Both the Beaver, SKEMP'-KUHL, and the Bear, TCHIHT'-WIHN, were totemic figures, but their physical counterparts were much prized for their rich furs. Also, while KLYE'-UHK, the Eagle, was a significant subject of ceremonial masks, the bird was hunted for certain of its feathers, the only ones that proved suitable for fletching arrows. SKWEET-OOL', the Raven, and TCHASS'-KHAIN, the Condor, mythological as well as actual creatures, were not hunted, nor was WOHK-AH-NATCH'-AHM, the Wolf, whose legendary being provided the novitiate with spirit power.

According to Basil Joe, the ancient Sechelt believed that the shag, a diving bird, would become human if skinned. The shag is closely related to a bird known in northern Europe as the guillemot, linguistically linked to the French word "guillaume," meaning "William." Celtic folklore says that certain birds shed their skins and become human in form.[3] Aboriginal Sechelt taboos against the eating of certain birds and animals coincide quite closely with those established in Biblical times among the Israelites.[4]

Fire for cooking was made by a process of twirling a dry cedar stick between the palms of the hands with the tip pressed against a dry cedar plank, near its edge. When a spark appeared, it was pushed into a small bit a dry shredded bark and carefully blown into a flame. This process, known as SKWAYS'-LATH-KOHP, has rarely been mastered by anyone who was not Indian. Basil Joe said that he managed it when young, with great effort, but that the most expert at it were women who had done this chore all of their lives.

While firemaking was a task performed generally by women, men also found the skill a useful one to know. Hunters, returning late along trails that wound at the bottom of steep valleys and through dense woods, sometimes had to resort to lighting pitch torches to find their way back to their village. For this emergency, bundles of slivers of pitchy wood were lashed to poles and cached at regular intervals along such trails. Obviously, the hunters would have to be able to ignite the first torch in order to light their way. More generally, however, these emergency torches were made use of by groups of both men and women who were caught by oncoming darkness while shuttling their dried berries, roots, and meat down the mountainside, in mid-September.

Reg Paull recalled that when, as a boy, he had accompanied hunters up the valley of TCHIM'-TCHIM, Hunachin Creek, at the head of Jervis Inlet, one of his uncles would peer into rock crevices here and there along the trail. Reg, curious, was told the reason for these old torches.

As firemaking was a painstaking process prior to the introduction of European matches, even with tinder-dry wood from the dead spires of mountain cedar, efforts were made to preserve it to save rekindling. The most common method, in lodges and at camps, was to bank fires so that embers could be fanned back into flames. The other, that introduced by the SPIHL'-AHM-OHSS of TAHK-WHOHT'-TSAIN, Saint Vincent Bay, consisted of lighting a slow-burning tinder packed between large clam shells, covered with clay. Fire thus preserved could be transported several hours and used, when a stopping place was reached, to kindle a camp-fire or a torch.

Cooking was done by barbecuing in pits, by frying on heated hearthstones, and by boiling in baskets or wooden boxes. Since such utensils could not withstand direct fire, water was brought to a boil through the insertion of hot rocks. Only fine-grained basalt was used, as this rock would not chip or affect the flavour of the food being cooked. Chowders and soups prepared in this manner were eaten by means of a large ladle, called a TCHAHW'-EYE, carved from goat horn or arbutus wood—the Madrona—and often decorated. Liquid foods were tilted into the mouth from this ladle carved in the form of an oval—the shape of plenty.

Herring, KWOY'-OHK, were generally caught in a net called a KLEHP-AHLK'. The net was spread out on the beach at low tide. When the rising water lifted the floats to which it was fastened, it prevented the fish that had swum over it from escaping. That the SPIHL'-AHM-OHSS at SAUGH-KWAH'-MAIN had brought the art of catching and curing eggs of the spawning herring, SUHSS'-KWAH, would seem to mark the bay of Pender Habour as age-old herring grounds.

A creek mouth about a mile below STAHTK-WHAY'-LAIN, Nine-Mile Point, became known as TCHEH-MUHM'-MAIN because it was a good place to obtain roe from this fish. Roe of the SUHSS'-KWAH was considered a delicacy. It was obtained by setting boughs under water during spawning season, then drawing them out when covered with the tiny rubbery eggs—a process known as TCHEH-MUHM'.

Herring were also caught by means of a KLUH-TUH'-MAIN, a flattened pole with spines of sharpened KAH'-LAH-KYE, ironwood, inserted along one edge. Non-Indian settlers quickly adopted this Native fishing device for their own use, inserting steel instead of wooden teeth along the working edge. Held flat, the rake served—and still serves—as a paddle to propel the fisherman's canoe or small boat through the water.

Herring and salmon were either cooked for immediate consumption or dried and smoked for future use. The English language has adopted the Sechelt name SAUGH'-EYE for a family of salmon. In the Sechelt language, SAUGH meant "full" and EYE meant "good." So the name of this prized fish meant, literally, "full of good." That the coho was also considered a tasty dish is attested to by the EYE syllable in its name, KUHM-EYE-YAYTS'-AH. HUHN'-OHN, the pink salmon, was a beautiful fish when it first arrived in July. The chum salmon, known as YAH'-NO-KWUH, while not so highly rated when cooked fresh, made an excellent smoked fish. The spring salmon, YEW'-MATCH, was also without the EYE syllable in its name, but was a highly prized variety of salmon. When taken to the winter lodge, smoked salmon was usually hung high up against the unceilinged roof, where it continually received additional preservative smoking from the central fire. Some Sechelt families have retained the art of drying a salmon so thoroughly that it is almost as thin as paper.

Three devices were employed by the Sechelt to catch salmon: the spear, the net, and the trap. The first of these, the SHEHL-AYL'-EH-TUHN, was made from yellow cedar and was, typically, about ten feet in length. Its throwing end was flattened to almost the width of a hand, and was indented with two half-circle fingergrips. Two prongs projected some eighteen inches beyond the main shaft-head, to which they were bound with bark of the KWUHT-NAY'-TSEYE, the wild cherry. This bark was then glazed with amber of the pine, the same polyester glue being used today with fiberglass. Over the tip of each of these prongs, a point was held in place by a leather thong that ran back to the main shaft. Each point was made from three pieces of deer antler bound together with cherry bark to form a tip at one end and a socket at the other. The bark binding the pieces of antler together was continually glazed by the hunter to keep its surface smooth.

This spear was used in deep water off creek and river mouths before the fish entered the fresh water. If a speared salmon were to thresh violently, the embedded harpoon tip, the SNAY'-NATCH, would twist free, saving the prong from breaking while remaining attached to the spear by its leather thong. A braided rope, attached to the spear by means of two specially slanted holes cut through it near its flattened end, permitted the thrower to retrieve the harpoon tip readily. In a particularly thick school, one SHEHL-AYL,[5] that is, one throw of the spear, might harpoon a fish on each of its two tips.

SLOH'-WUHL, a finely braided twine or rope made from the inner, sap-bearing bark of the red cedar was used to make the SLOH-WUHL'-TUHN, the salmon net. Nets were suspended from logs in likely places, such as MAHL-MOH'-LOHM, up-inlet from Deserted Bay and a quarter mile or so above and offshore from TEHL-TUHL-WAHN'. Here, so the Sechelt say, a spring of fresh water boils up through the salt water. The term MAHL-MOH'-LOHM was a name imitative of the sound made by bubbling water.

Early white settlers at Gibson's landing, known to the Sechelt as KYE-AH-TAH'-WAHN, believed that good fishing around what became known as Salmon Rock resulted from the fact that fish were attracted to this pot by fresh water springs deep under the sea there. In all likelihood, this belief was learned from members of the Squamish Native people, a number of whom befriended the West Howe Sound newcomers who were striving to "Live off the land."[6]

Traps varied in detail but, in general, they followed a plan by which fish were permitted to enter but not to leave. One trap that served this purpose was the LOH'-LOH-UH, a piling trap. Stubs of old pilings, exposed at the mouth of the TSOH'-NYE at Deserted Bay by a storm about 1950 showed that the people had trapped fish with a weir constructed in the form of a double "J," one on each side of the river. Fish could enter between the backs of the "J's" at high tide, but those that remained too long within the curves of the traps were stranded as the waters receded.

In the late 1960s, when the Porpoise Bay beach was dredged along the course of the marsh stream that flows on to it near the wharf, a great trap, hundreds of feet in length, was dug up. The posts had been sharpened, and they had been closely interwoven with braided bands of cedar bark to form two fences, gradually converging, from below low water to near the top of the beach.

Somewhat similar to the piling trap in shape, but constructed of rocks laid to form a groin, was the LOH'-UHLTH. One such structure, now much eroded by logging operations, was built in ancient times on the beach below the stream that drains SAUGH'-AH-NAH. Another, more like an open "U," exists still in Boom Bay, immediately up Agamemnon Channel from there. It has also been eroded by log action.

Another trap, the KWAYT'-LATCH, consisted of a large, loosely woven basket with a flat bottom and one open end. This open end was immersed in an eddy of a salmon stream. Fish, encountering the basket's sloping surface, sometimes flipped out on to the portion remaining above water.

Still another salmon trap, the MAH'-TSLAH, consisted of a conical-shaped basket, woven from young cedar roots. It was modelled in such a way that fish could enter the large lower end, but could neither proceed upstream nor return through the tapered entrance; a principle on which lobster and crab trap construction around the world had been based from ages past.

Almost every stream maintained a run of some variety of salmon until well into the twentieth century. Elderly Sechelt women used to say that some runs were created by their people in olden times, by planting and fertilizing roe in gravel beds of these streams. They said that during their childhood, around the turn of the century, women who were old at that time would maintain this planting of spawn. The sockeye run into SAUGH'-AH-NAH, they said, was the doing of their people – made possible by the clearing away of boulders which once clogged the stream entrance. They had also, they said, brought fish of this species into the slough at Porpoise Bay, they said, until it was ruined by an earth fill. Years ago, people far inland carried spawning salmon above falls so that others still farther inland could have food. While these stories cannot be verified today, their basic message remains. For although Native Indians drew heavily on every stream for salmon to smoke for winter months, they depleted none of these spawning grounds of their prolific runs.

Trout, SKAY'-KOO-UH, were fished in streams with rod and line. Instead of a hook, the Sechelt attached to their lines salmon eggs entangled in human hair. Fish could be kept fresh for as long as three days, even during warm weather, so it was said, if wrapped and packed in selected sea-weed.

The Sechelt recognized and used a number of varieties of clam. The common clam was called SKWAH-EYE'-EE. The horse clam, similar to the common clam but larger, was SMUHT'-EYE; and the butter clam was called KWAHT-EYE'-AHM. From the fact that each of these names contains the expression EYE, we can infer that the clam was considered good. The word for cockle, SKUHL'-OHM, a crustacean of tougher fiber, lacks the EYE in its name. Oysters were unknown in olden times.

"I like clams," said Basil Joe, seated on the fabulously rich bed at NEE'-AHM-ISH, in Narrows Arm. "I like them boiled, or fried, or raw," he continued, suiting act to word by downing a specimen straight from the shell.

As Basil indicated, clams were eaten raw, fried, or boiled. Cockles were prepared by being boiled for a long period of time, then strung on sticks of KAH'-LAH-KYE, the ironwood, and smoked.

Many sites derived Sechelt names from clams or cockles that

were to be found in these localities. KWAHT-EYE'-AHM, midway up LEAL'-KO-MAIN, Agamemnon Channel, is so called because it is the site of the Sechelt's most succulent bed of butter clams. In Sechelt Inlet, KLAYT-LOH'-MAH, SLAUGH-AH'-MAIN, and SLAUGH-WIHK'-AHM-EYE were good beds of cockles, large mussels, and small mussels, respectively. The large mussels were called SLAUGH'-OH-KWOHM. SLAY-OHTH-KWOHT'-AHM, a pool behind a reef at the south entrance to Storm Bay, SHARK'-AIN, means, "It can be bailed out, and then there are lots of clams." NEE'-AHM-ISH, also known as SEE-AY'-AH-NESS, on the upcoast entrance to Narrows Arm, has already been alluded to. AY'-UHL-KHAIN, at the head of Blind Bay, AH'-TAH-LAITH, remains a choice butter clam bed. Scores of other smaller beds were known and used, and some still produce seafoods for any who wish to dig them.

Piles of discarded clam and cockle shells form the sole evidence, near these former food-gathering spots, of the presence of the aboriginal people. At SAUGH-KWAH'-MAIN, Garden Bay, acres of grounds where winter lodges once stood remained a continuous midden, several feet in depth, until the site was subdivided. Logging operations and building developments have erased many of the marks left by timeless accumulations of sea shells. Some identified midden sites have suffered little damage.

Seals, porpoises, and sea lions were taken by harpoons. The seal, AHSK, was sought at its den, called by the Sechelt AHSK'-AHM-MAIN. The most common method of hunting this sea mammal was to entice it from its den by throwing pebbles into the water. In the belief, most likely, that these tiny objects were small fish, the seal emerged from its den. As it rose slowly to the surface, where it had to seek air at intervals, the hunter, waiting quietly in his canoe above, speared it with his TCHEE'-TCHOSS, a single-pronged harpoon with a detachable head. The original model of this weapon had been brought to KAL-PAY'-LAIN at the dawn of time by the SPIHL'-AHM-OHSS set down there.

The typical seal den was located in a cave, formed by some ancient slide of boulders, with its interior above sea level and its entrance below sea level. The Indians learned of these dens from close observation, and knew where to go to find the creatures, who were too alert and quick to be taken in open water.

One of the best known dens, the name of which was generally contracted by the Sechelt to KUHM'-MAIN, is located on the left shore of SMAIT, Hotham Sound, about three miles from its head. Another, at HOH-PAHL'-SHEEN, is to be found three miles below Brittain River; another at YAH'-NO-WHOHM, immediately north of the mouth of Glacier Creek.

A good seal hunter was brave enough to dive and enter the KUHM'-MAIN itself, if necessary, killing his prey there and swimming out with it. The Sechelt maintain that this hazardous method was practised up to modern times.

Just below Thornhill Point, in SKOO'-PAH, Salmon Arm, a traditional seal den was located beneath huge granite boulders. Here, hunters could sometimes harpoon seals from above, through an opening in the slide. Bennie Joe, who spent some years of his boyhood in the vicinity of this den, said that young children were forbidden to play among its boulders, lest they fall down this opening and drown.

The seal's meat was important to the Sechelt's diet. It's hide made leather thongs, and its bladder could be used as a container for oil. The animal figured prominently in conventional adornment of wooden artifacts and utensils.

The porpoise, KWOH'-NOHT, was also harpooned from a canoe; but it had to be lured alongside the vessel, since it had no accessible den. An artful hunter learned to do this trick by appealing to the creature's susceptibility to certain sounds, and to his love of mimicry and play. Through the skilful whistling of extremely highly pitched notes, the hunter succeeded in luring his prize close enough to harpoon it.

Dan Johnson, noted hunter of SAUGH-KWAH'-MAIN during the early 1900s, could apparently lure not only KWOH'-NOHT, the porpoise, but also STAH'-LAH-SHAN, the killer whale, with supersonic whistling notes. His grandson, Andy Johnson, has said that Dan would sometimes entice a pod of killer whales into a fleet of gill netters at Rivers Inlet, much to the consternation of the fishermen. When his whistling ceased, the whales would proceed on their way without having harmed the nets.

A whistle, TCHAY-AH-MUHM'-MAIN, made from a thin strip of inner bark of the red cedar, was blown against to create a bleating deer call. Variations of technique in blowing against the fine edge of the TCHAY-AH-MUHM'-MAIN may have also created the sounds required to lure the porpoise to the hunter's spear.

Meat of the porpoise was generally barbecued, wrapped in specially selected seaweed – a process known as TAY'-PYE. Reg Paull recalled having eaten, as a boy, barbecued KWOH'-NOHT that had been caught by the late Dan Johnson, one of the last skilled in the hunting of these creatures. Reg said that it tasted delicious. The legend of the hunter who was pulled from his canoe by a harpooned porpoise and drowned, and who then entered its sea kingdom in spirit, would seem to indicate a rather unusual affinity to this fascinating creature among the aboriginal Sechelt people.[7]

Two localities, Nevill Rock, off Evenden Point at the western entrance to Jervis Inlet; and White Islands, off Wilson Creek, were named KWAH-KAH-NAYSS'-AHM by the Sechelt from KWAH-KAH-NAYSS', their name for the sea lion. A hunter trained in the exacting ritual of stalking these huge sea beasts would have ranked high among his people's nobility. The hunter would swim among the sea lions, imitating their movements, as they sported near one of their favourite haunts. Clasped beneath his arm, he carried a TSHEE'-TCHOSS, a heavy javelin. Fastened to the detachable head of the javelin was a rope of bark, nettle, or leather which trailed behind the hunter to his companions on the rock. These people would observe the hunt, yet remain concealed form view. When sufficiently close to a selected member of the herd, the hunter would skilfully thrust the weapon home, then swim quickly from the turmoil. The men anchoring the rope would play the harpooned monster until it could be dispatched.

That bristles from the KWAH-KAH-NAYSS' were frequently placed in chiefs' headpieces gives an indication of the respect Native Indians held for this tremendously powerful creature, and of the degree of difficulty and danger involved in overcoming one.

Hunting of the mountain goat, SWAYT'-LYE, has already been mentioned here. To qualify as a hunter, the young aristocratic male was obliged to "get his goat." Success depended on both agility and skill. Even after the ritual bathing, the hunter must take care that he stalk his game from the lee side. In order to achieve this advantage, he needed to know not only the direction of horizontal winds, but also courses of air currents along the vertical sides of mountains.

Long years before the Hudson's Bay blanket became a unit of exchange across the North American continent, the Sechelt were making use of the mountain goat blanket, the SWOH'-KWOTH, as their unit of wealth. Made from the long winter coat of this animal, the blanket was both warm and durable. The Sechelt say that their ancestors did not weave their yarn, but knitted it into whatever form they wished to produce. Original Cowichan sweaters, they say, were knitted with a stitch adapted from the Sechelt SWOH'-KWOTH, dating back to times when this blanket was traded to Vancouver Island peoples in exchange for shells and other items from the west coast.

The most popular game animal was the deer, HOH'-PAYT. Almost every part of this animal could be put to some use. In addition to providing meat, leather, bone for arrows, and antlers for harpoon tips, the spinal cord of a mature buck could, for instance, be made into a bowstring unaffected by weather changes.

The hunter usually took along his TCHIHN'-OO, his hunting dog, to aid him. This animal–part wolf–had been bred and trained to work with his master. Basil Joe said that these dogs were not large, but that they were exceptionally good at hunting. His father's dogs, he said, would go into the woods and chase the deer to where the hunter was waiting.

A hunter, in setting out with his dogs, would say that he was going YUHK-WUHM'; that is, that he would remain in his canoe while his dogs drove deer to him. One of these dogs whose name survives was TCHEE'-LEE, "good hunter." Another, PAHP'-WHAHM, "modest one," was also named after his predominant quality, highly praised by the Sechelt in a dog as well as in a human being. He excelled in hunting, but he did not boast of his prowess. The hunter's main, or "hero" dog, he would refer to, so Reg Paull said, as his LAHK-EYE'. These dogs drove only buck deer. Clarence Joe said that TCHEE'-LEE was so fast and powerful that a weight had to be hung about his neck to prevent his overtaking and killing the deer far away from his master.

One very popular spot where the hunter's dog could help him was SWAH'-WAHP, part way up Hotham Sound. Here, just inside Saint Vincent Bay from Elephant Point, a wooded island is separated from the mainland by a series of reefs. Flushed from the island, the deer could be picked off by a bowman, STUHM-TOH'-MISH, stationed where it would attempt to reach shore.

The Sechelt term STUHM-TOH'-MISH, for bowman, or archer, found its way, as did its equivalent among the ancient Greeks, into astronomy. About six distinct sizes of bow were used, the largest of which could be pulled only by the strongest archers, the STUHM-TOH'-MISH. The arrow, HYE-EYE'-TUHN, varied in size with the bow. Bird arrows were tipped with split deer-bone. Larger ones for use on game animals were tipped with various sizes, shapes, and kinds of rock – some of chipped flint; others of sharpened slate.

To avoid having to carry large numbers of shafts, the hunter usually embedded his big game arrowheads lightly. When an arrow struck a deer of other game creature, the head would penetrate and the shaft would fall free, preventing it from breaking against trees when the animal ran. Feathers–usually two– were bound to the shaft at the quill. They were then bent forward at a slight angle and the tips were bound. The twist gave the arrow a spin in flight, adding accuracy.

Sometimes the hunt took the form of AH'-MAH-KLATH. This meant that the hunter intended to bring back meat for old persons, who could not go out on their own.

In addition to gathering and hunting foods, at some villages the Sechelt maintained gardens, PUHN-NUHM'-MAIN, where wild plants were cared for and harvested.

Roots and tubers that required cool storage were kept in a root cellar, a PUHN'-AHWTWUH–the same term used to designate a burial place and a ceremonial cave.

Despite the usual abundance of game and fish, natural cataclysms, excessive snowfalls, and population increases among predators combined during certain years to bring famine, KWYE-TIHM-SHISH-AHL'-AH-MOHT. Basil Joe said that his people had suffered from famine as recently as the time of his youth, when during one year no fish of any species were available.

The most fearsome creature accosted by the Indian hunter was MY'-OOK, the grizzly, largest of the TCHIHT'-WIHN, the bear family. Not only was this beast fantastically powerful, but he was also mean and intelligent–a most awesome combination of characteristics.

That the ablest Sechelt STUHM-TOH'-MISH fought this dreadful creature is alluded to in their astronomy, in which the bowman aims at a MY'-OOK target. Fighting the MY'-OOK is the basis of one of their most fascinating hunting stories.

Three brothers were paddling up the TSOH'-NYE River with their dog on a hunting expedition. According to Clarence Joe, who told the story, these men were among his ancestors. They were, so the tale relates, huge, powerful, young men. Their wrists were as wide as an average man's palm. No ordinary hand could go round one of their paddles. No ordinary archer could pull one of their bows.

Suddenly, as they rounded a turn in the river, they came upon a grizzly. One of the elder brothers sent an arrow into it. Wounded, it plunged off through the woods. The youngest brother sprang ashore with his dog and set off in pursuit, while the other two brothers remained to watch for signs of the animal from the canoe.

Employing his typical cunning, the wounded bear leaped from a hiding spot on to the young hunter, who had been following the grizzly's tracks in a light snow. The bear then pinned him between two small fallen trees. Thrusting a thumb into each corner of its mouth, and pressing out with his tremendously powerful arms, the young man was able to prevent the monster from using its teeth on him. The two trees protected his body from a crushing bear hug, but not from the creature's claws.

At the moment of the ambush, the hunter's dog had run back to where the two older brothers waited. Sensing trouble, they immediately set out with him back to the scene of the struggle. The oldest brother ran up to the bear, felt for a vulnerable spot behind the shoulder blade, leapt back, and sent an arrow into one and then into the other of the beast's sides. With the second, it collapsed dead.

The hunters carried the younger brother to the river, which ran red with his blood when they bathed his wounds. Back at their home village of TSOH'-NYE he was treated with a solution made from KWIHN'-ASTH, the healing mountain hellebore, and he recovered from the terrible encounter.

Clarence Joe said that this tale was told soon after the birth of his first son, William, by the newborn's paternal great-grandfather, who held the boy on his knee during the telling. The story was the family's property. Upon its completion, he named the child, not after one of his illustrious ancestors, as was the usual custom, but after the worthy adversary, MY' OOK.

While seemingly a story, this account could well be a mythical reference to the three SPIHL'-AHM-OHSS, "First Man" brothers who brought the art of weaponry "from the sky" to TSOH'-NYE, the locale of this fearsome combat.[9]

Chapter Ten

Probably nowhere else did Earth's human inhabitants feel a closer affinity to other creatures of nature than among the aborigines of the northwest coast of North America. The Indian was conscious of his nakedness, because he frequently went unclothed. He was conscious also of the superior strength of many land and sea animals, conquest of which taxed his group ingenuity to the utmost. The Indian pictured all living beings about him literally as his fellows.

As did other peoples of the Northwest culture, the Sechelt fashioned for use almost everything they touched. Not only did they cut, chop, split, and bore with stone and bone implements, they also made the implements themselves. All hunters learned to fashion the weapons of their profession; the bow, SLUHK, and the arrow, HYE-EYE'-TUHN. In like manner, fishermen custom-made their own hooks, AH'-WAYL, and spears, SHEHL-AYL'-TUHN, and maintained these essential implements.

Arrowheads, SNAY'-NATCH, of flint, KAH-PEELTH'-PYE, were used rough and unpolished. They were expendable, and the hunter could quickly chip out new ones. The arrow shaft, in contrast, was made smooth from end to end. Fashioned by the KOH'-TOH-TSAIN, a narrow drawknife with a blade of ironwood, burned hard, the shaft was smoothed by being drawn along a groove or through a hole in a special type of stone. TCHATH-LAITH'-TUHN, the stone hammer, was brought to a smooth, polished surface, not only where it would be gripped by the hand, but also over the remainder of the implement. Some of Sechelt manufacture were flat on top; others were brought to a rounded tip, which occasionally was cleft. Most hammers were fashioned from some form of andesite or nephrite, quite compact and tough stones; but a few have been found that were made from granite.

The pestle-shaped hammer with a cleft tip inevitably evokes phallic symbolism. However, since a single site may produce a variety of styles, the possibility of hereditary, heraldic imagery, similar to what appeared in the carving of other objects, must also be considered. A high percentage of hammers, even among those fashioned from the hardest granite, have been found in fragments with rounded tips destroyed, often among other stone objects still intact. One theory is that aboriginal stone hammers had their place in the mythical as well as the physical world, and that many were broken deliberately when the old way of life came to an end.[1]

The adze, KYE-AH-TCHAY'-MAIN, was invariably polished all over like the hammer, not only on the blade. With only stone to erode stone, the craftsman would grind one surface of the blade perfectly flat and leave the other side slightly rounded. If he found a vein of jade in the process, he would use this strip as the cutting edge, for it was much harder than the jadeite that constituted most of the piece. At certain spots in Sechelt Inlet, particularly at KWAHT-AHM'-OHSS near Egmont, and at SWAY'-KALS in Porpoise Bay, adze blades of pure jade have been recovered. Since there is no known source of jade along the Lower Mainland coast, however, it is suggested by present-day Sechelt that these articles may have been transported here by a group of Lillooet who stayed among these coastal neighbours during the 1850s[2] and that the articles were perhaps traded by these people. When mounted on a "D" handle or at the butt of a springy limb, the head wrapped in deerhide for resilience, the adze blade made an effective woodworking tool. Reg Paull's adze heads, though made of steel, were joined to handles, TCHIHN-TCHIHN'-EYE, which were cut from the dogwood tree, SLAHL-SHIHM'-NYE, in the traditional manner.

Women fashioned weaving needles, TCHEW-STAH'-MAIN, from the ironwood, KAH'-LAH-KYE. The needles were up to thirty inches long, eyed at one end and brought to a rounded spatulate tip on the other. With these slightly curved shafts, they wove lengths of cured bulrushes, SAH-SWAIL'-NAT, into very soft and resilient mats, TSHUHM'-OHT-EHN, and sleeping mats, TSLAY'-WHOY.

In 1965, Reg Paul obtained some carving tools used by SLUHK'-TUHN, last patriarch of Saltery Bay, along with a TSLAY'-WHOY woven by his wife, KAH-KEE'-ATH. Although at least half a century old, the mat retained its resiliency.

From single sheets of cedar bark, TSOH'-KWOHM, women fashioned bailing pots, TSOH'-KWOHM-MAIN. They were shaped to fit the bottom of a canoe, and were lashed at either end of a cedar-slat handle by ribbons of the inner layer of cedar bark.

Where a red cedar tree, TUH-HUHM'-EYE, grew on hardpan or in shallow soil above rock, the basket maker grubbed out some of its trailing roots as raw materials for her work. To prepare the root, she would peel it, then split away the outer, sapwood layer. She would then trim strips from this pliable sapwood ring which were as long as possible and of consistent width and thickness—much the shape of the present-day flat shoelace.

In coiled basketry, the maker would wind a strip of root, its natural surface outermost, around a tiny bundle of slivers split from the inner root. As with the weavers of the Panama hat, far to the south, the Sechelt basket maker worked her cedar-root strip directly from a container of water in which it had been allowed to soak.

To begin her coil, she would push an awl under a lace of the inner round, through which she would thread the sharpened point of her strip. She would then pull it, as pliable as leather, through the opening so as to bind one coil to the other. Slivers were inserted as required to maintain an even core. Lacing was invisibly lapped over the end of the previous strip as needed to make a continuous length.

When the bottom of the basket had reached its desired diameter, the basket maker made a coil atop the outer edge, and continued to build upwards in the same manner until she reached the height she wished. A lid might be made in the same way, constructed so that the end of the outer coil could be butted against the end of the basket's top coil. Such a basket, made by an expert, could be used to hold liquids, and as a cooking utensil.

If the basket maker needed a less compact product than the coil basket, she could lace her root strips around thin slats of split cedar, made pliable through soaking in hot water. Whichever method was used, basket making involved a stitching rather than a weaving technique. With the tip of the material forming its own needle, the basket was literally sewn. The basket maker created a design on her product by imbricating strips of cherry bark and blanched reeds into her stitching.

The aboriginal Sechelt used no unit of measurement; neither did they make use of any sort of measuring device. Symmetry in the shape of the basket and its decorations, which must be interposed during the stitching process, could be attained only by the artist's hands responding to the eye.[3] The completed work had to be visualized in its entirety from the beginning.

A basket maker would not imitate any motif of another artist, nor would she repeat any of her own designs. Each basket became a unique production.

A basket made for carrying a baby was called a POHT'-SOHTH. A basket with a lid was a KAHK'-TCHAH. To carry berries and tubers, two baskets, one above the other, were fastened to a piece of cedar-bark matting. This device, known as a SPIHT'-YOO, was tied about the waist and suspended from the forehead by a tump-strap, a KAHT'-LAH. It placed one basket between the shoulders and one at the hips.

While all of the foregoing involved fashioning finished products from raw materials, none of these processes were considered carving by the Sechelt. Anyone could HYE'-EYE; that is, could make something. The name for the arrow, HYE-EYE'-TUHN, for instance, means literally "something made."

The true carver was designated by the name HUHT'-KWOHM. This man—usually an aristocrat, a member of the KWAHT-KWAHT-AHM'—not only made objects but often adorned them with traditional stylistic figures cut into the wood.

As he carved, the HUHT'-KWOHM would chant time-honoured secret incantations, literally carving his songs of the spirit world into his work. Known to the Sechelt as TSEE-YOO'-UHT, this mystic art resembled very closely the process by which magical words were hammered into swords and pieces of armor at the time of the legendary Arthur.

Almost all carving was made from either TUH-HUHM'-EYE, the red cedar, or TEY'-KWOY, the yellow cedar. The main items considered by the Sechelt to be HUHT'-KWOHM-MAIN; literally, "carved by hand," were canoes, bowls, chests, ceremonial paddles, lodgeposts, totem poles, staffs, and masks. To a certain extent, every member of the KWAHT-KWAHT-AHM' was a HUHT'-KWOHM. All aristocratic males could make paddles, chests, and staffs, and could ornament them with personal and hereditary figures.

Invariably, these figures were drawn from the animated world of mythology. Thus, while a carved staff or a pole might realistically depict figures of a snake, a beaver, a condor, or a killer whale, it simultaneously symbolized TCHAIN'-KO, SKEMP'-KOOL, TCHASS'-KHAIN, and STAH'-LAH-SHAN, respectively. The "story" that such a carved object "told" generally came from the realm of mythology and legend.

Some of the symbols carved portrayed creatures which existed only in mythology; others, those which existed in both the real and the legendary world. Among the latter group represented in Pacific Northwest carvings were the Raven, known to the Sechelt as SKWEET-OOL'; the Mink, known as KYE'-AHKS; the Wolf, known as WOHK-AH-NATCH'-AHM; the Bear, known as TCHIHT'-WIHN; and the Eagle, known as KLYE'-UHK.

Some creatures were assigned dual names, according to their role in either the actual or the mythological world. The long-necked loon, for instance, which elderly Sechelt say still nests around SAUGH-AH-LAY'-AHM, now called Green Bay, was known as LAY'-AHM. The nesting place SAUGH-AH-LAY'-AHM means, literally, "full of loons." Mythological loon, however, was referred to as KAH'-AH-MOHL. In like manner, the ordinary owl was called HAY'-UHK-AHN'-AYK, while the Owl of legend was designated OH'-KWOHM.

The Thunderbird, whom the Sechelt referred to as KWAHT-KAY'-AHM; and the Serpent, TCHAIN'-KO — mythological lords of the sky and sea, respectively — seem not to have been based entirely on any specific real creatures, and were common symbols along this coast. To these, the Sechelt added a third symbolic figure, the TCHAY'-TAY-LAITCH.

The TCHAY'-TAY-LAITCH presents an interesting example of the thin borderline between the mythical and the real that so baffles the Western mind when it attempts to understand aboriginal lore. The nearest equivalent to this term would probably be found in the expression "Good Luck Charm."

A paddler, travelling near the shoreline of lake or inlet, might hear a sound like the cry of a baby. If he desired good fortune, he must proceed quietly ashore where, usually, he could find the TCHAY'-TAY-LAITCH. He would carry the creature home, wrap it carefully in soft hair of the SWAYT'-LYE, the mountain goat, and place it gently in his WIHK'-AHM, his regalia chest. The traveller must let no one know of his find.

Should he carry out this procedure, he would do well in his undertakings: he would catch YOH'-MATCH, the salmon; he would bring home meat of HOH'-PAYT, the deer. If a hunter or a fisherman seemed to be always successful, people would say to one another, "He must have a TCHAY'-TAY-LAITCH."

Should someone who had found a TCHAY'-TAY-LAITCH let it be known, the creature would disappear and, with it, his good luck. Sometimes, the creature of good fortune would cry from deep within a rocky cliff, where it had the power to hide itself. In this case, the seeker could not find it. Thereafter, he would be "through"; he would be "no good"; "all washed up," so to speak.

While, supposedly, few ever found a TCHAY'-TAY-LAITCH, and while no one who had found one revealed his find, the Sechelt assigned a shape and a coloration to this good omen. Carvers portrayed it in a form very much like that of a frog, painted green, and spotted. The late Dan Paull, hereditary carver, placed the likeness of this legendary creature at the base of many of his poles.

TCHAIN'-KO, god of the sea, was also assigned a shape–that of the universal Dragon. Sometimes, as in the twined figure near KLAYK-NAYK'-OHLT, the bay of Misery Creek, he has sight. In the pole already referred to, carved by Reg Paull, he is portrayed blind. Aristocrats often made use of this powerful symbol wound about their staffs of authority; their "talking sticks."

Far back in time, representations of both actual and mythical creatures became conventional. A HUHT'-KWOHM could not substitute one symbolic figure for another at will. He could, however, add a personal touch to accepted forms. For instance, Frank Eugene, a carver from KLAY'-AH-KWOHSS, who worked early in this century, depicted TCHASS'-KHAIN, the Condor, atop his poles with head down and wings folded. The late Rennie John, HUHT'-KWOHM, descended from HUHN'-AH-TCHIN chiefs, displayed the wings outstretched. Reg Paull, hereditary TAHW-AHN'-KWUH carver, raised the wings as if he wished to show the mythical bird about to fly.

Ages ago, carving became both a class and a hereditary function. Only the members of the KWAHT-KWAHT-AHM', the aristocracy, could carve presentation paddles, SKWAH'-KWEE-AHM; and could carve and wear ceremonial masks, SKWAY'-AH-KWOY. Although the village way of life and its class structure has long ago broken down insofar as any legal status is concerned, traditional hereditary rights and privileges are still maintained to a considerable extent. Family pedigrees are kept track of, and hereditary rights to carve certain poles, masks, and staffs are recognized.

All carving seemed to dwell in a realm of mysticism. Present-day commentators like to refer to aboriginal carvings and paintings as the work of "artists." But no Western artist could find a world today so peopled with culturally accepted spirits as the world known to the ancient Sechelt. Immersed in an environment governed as much by spiritual as by natural forces, the aboriginal carver created objects that reflected both mystic and natural visions. Born into a duality, the true meaning of which had already been long lost in Mediterranean cultures even by Plato's time, these carvings cannot now be judged by any criteria whatever that a modern critic might think appropriate for his evaluations. While no extraneous cultural patterns existed to bring doubt and confusion, critics and their value judgements were not necessary because viewers, themselves immersed in the carver's spiritual world, understood his intentions spiritually, if not actually.

The YOO-WAHSS, the canoe maker, worked in a particular world of spirituality. During the making of a war canoe, a KWAY'-NAY-AYTH, especially, he was obliged to live in accordance with quite strict rules of behaviour during crucial stages in the steaming and spreading of the great log. Any inappropriate act or thought, even by some other member of his family, might cause the wood to split or warp.

The making of the KWAY'-NAY-AYTH demanded the most rigid attention to time-honoured procedures. First, a huge cedar tree must be felled. This tree must grow in a sheltered valley, shaded from the sun so that its fibres were not twisted by direct sunshine. With the use of wedges made from wood of the yew, WHAH-WHAYT'-EYE, the trunk must then be split in half.

The YOO'-WAHSS began to work with his half log lying flat, on its heart, and the rounded side uppermost. Outside wood was chopped away with the KYE-AH-TCHAY'-MAIN to the desired shape. Inside wood was first burned out, the fire controlled by wet sand, then adzed.

To ensure accurate thickness on the sides and bottom of the canoe, the carver drove slivers of hard wood through the hull from the outside. He then chopped carefully on the inside until he reached the tips of these markers. Apart from these gauges, no measuring devices of any kind were used in the construction of this intricate piece of work. All symmetry was attained by the eye of the carver. Should the finished product reveal any quirk in its lines, it was believed that the YOO'-WAHSS must have been afflicted by some natural or spiritual malady during the making of this particular part.

To obtain maximum use of the wood the carver made the hull comparatively narrow. Now, when all else was ready, it must be spread. The process was accomplished by steaming the wood for several days, while covered with leaves and boughs, and then springing the opening to take thwarts of increasing lengths. If all went well – if no spirits had been outraged – the canoe now assumed its final shape. A raised sternpiece and a projecting prow might now be sewn to the hull by means of laces split from roots of the spruce tree, TCHAYTH'-PYE.

A war canoe was launched with as much ceremony as now attends the launching of a battleship or an ocean liner.[4]

Several other types of canoe were made. While they did not require the exacting spreading process demanded of the war canoe, their construction still called upon the utmost skill of the YOO'-WAHSS. Without mould or template, the carver must create a product no only symmetrical, but also practical. Should there be a faulty line or curve, the vessel would not fulfill the requirements of performance demanded of it.

A canoe designed for speed, to be used for hunting seals, was called SNUH-KWIHT'-OOL. A fishing canoe was known as SNAYN'-HAY-WITH-AHM, and a family canoe, with high "foxnose" prow[5] to take rough weather, was named KYE'-UH-KWAYTH.

The most common paddle was the SKUHM'-OHL, made from wood of the maple tree, SKUHM'-OHL-EYE. Obviously, one of these two names was derived from the other. War canoe paddles, since they might be needed as weapons, were made of yew, WHAH-WHAYT'-EYE, a strong, hard, and heavy wood. The ceremonial paddle, SKWAH'-KWEE-AHM, made from yellow cedar, was not put to regular use.

When a ceremonial occasion necessitated the transport of large contingents of guests, villages might resort of the KAH'-NOH, devised by laying planks across two large canoes.

Aboriginal Sechelt gave names to six various winds that might affect their canoe travel. Worst was the cold winter north wind, STOH-LAH-MAY'-LAHK. Another rough wind was the southeaster, KWAY-WHAH'-LAHK. The west wind, KLAY-SHEE-AH'-LAHK, which blew mainly during summer months, was looked upon as a forerunner of good weather. During travel up-inlet, the KLUH-TAH'-LAHK proved favourable. For down-inlet travel, the KLUH-KOH-MAH'-LAHK was best. A fisherman setting out toward the Strait of Georgia, TSAIN'-KO, in an early summer morning, would sometimes have a gentle offshore wind, SLAH-LAH-SHAH'-LAHK, to aid him.

Just as spirits of certain creatures augmented the carver's spiritual life, the physical representations of these creatures contributed to his physical existence. A HUHT'-KWOHM, then, might visualize a creature used by his people for food as literally presenting a food bowl to the diner.

Reg Paull, hereditary carver, mentioned having seen such a bowl still in use during his boyhood, in the home of his grandfather, WHAIL'-KO. The heads of four seals, the AHSK, according to Reg's description, protruded from beneath the bowl. These creatures were carrying the bowl; but the bowl was not part of the creatures themselves. A polished limestone bowl from Persia at the time of Darius, now in the Guennol Collection in New York, is similar to its Sechelt counterpart in that the fore parts of eight lions appear to bear it on their backs.

There was a fine art to creating parts of a work which maintained their individuality while participating in and contributing to the effect of the finished whole. The art was pursued to a high degree of perfection by the Sechelt. In some parts of the world, stylized figures were in no sense freed from the material in which they were depicted. The Salish strove to give to their carved spirit-creatures a degree of individuality that suggested free moral agency.

Figures represented on the totem poles of the late Dan Paull, SKWAH-TCHEE'-OOLT, son of WHAIL'-KO, were developed in such detail, and were so nearly freed from their basic medium, that they convey individual personalities. At the same time, the figures are inescapable participants in the story depicted by the carver. Poles carved by Reg Paull, Dan's son, followed the family tradition in their indication of naturalistic features. Even in miniature figures, only three or four inches high, done by the late Rennie John, every tooth stands sharp and clear.

In later years, the HUHT'-KWOHM and the YOO'-WAHSS painted as well as carved their pieces. The Sechelt say, though, that the arts of making and of painting were once separated. The painter, they say, was known as YOH'-YOH-TLUHM, and his painting—on canoe, mask, or pole—was called YOH'-TLUHM.

Seventy years into the twentieth century, Reg Paull, carver-painter, still maintained what he said were traditional and hereditary colours in his work. Each conventional carving, Reg said, demanded a particular colour for each symbol carved into it. From a spectrum of red, yellow, green, and blue, in addition to black and white, the YOH'-YOH-TLUHM must select five colours for a particular mask or pole, and perhaps six for another.[6] Similar colours never bordered each other, but were kept apart by a pattern imposed by the HUHT'-KWOHM or the YOO'-WAHSS.

The Sechelt people have thus seen their myths made manifest in wood by a continuous succession of hereditary carvers.[7]

According to Basil Joe, several miles up the SKWAH'-KAH River, and high up a mountain above the southern shore of a lake, aboriginal Sechelt found pieces of copper lying free in its native state. So pure was this metal, SKWAY'-AH-KWAY, that it could be pounded and twisted into shape to form bracelets, TSOH'-AHT, and other ornaments.

Reg Paull said that, according to information told him by elders at the time of his youth, Sechelt metal workers would add powdered zinc blend to molten copper to make brass greaves, breastplates, and other pieces of armor. When iron became available, the working of this metal was called TSOH'-KOH-MAIN.

Aboriginal Sechelt named the present Dacres Point, in Narrows Arm, WAHL'-WAHL, after a special rock, so named, which was to be found there. Naturally formed in thin layers, WAHL'-WAHL was tough enough to be ground into tiny disks. These pieces were then punctured by a drill, KWAYT'-TSOH-MAIN, for the making of necklaces. Although similar in shape to the Atlantic coast wampum, the stone pieces were not used as money, Basil Joe said. About two thousand stone beads have been discovered by the Franske family immediately across Highway 101 from the Davis Bay Wharf.

One piece of carving in stone depicts a tragic story, according to one version of its origin. A boy, who was an only son, lived with his parents at KAY'-KAH-LAH-KUHM, now known as Selma Park. When he was old enough to range about on his own for short distances, the boy one day walked along the beach to the west. At TCHAK'-AHM, the creek mouth at Wakefield, he surprised a band of renegades from the north, waiting there for darkness to conceal their attack on the village. They killed the boy but did not attack the village. Through the loss of his life, the boy saved his home village from greater slaughter.

When the mother of the boy learned of her loss, she threw herself, so the story goes, from the top of the rocky bluff at the point where the breakwater touches shore now. Only the father, SLAHL-AHK-EYE'-MAHN, survived the family tragedy.

A carver, this story concludes, sculptured the mother holding her son, not as he was at the time of his death, but as a young child. Long after the statuette was lost, the story was passed along. Finally, early in the twentieth century the stone was recovered, when the ground at the old village site was being levelled. Now in the Vancouver Museum, it is about twenty inches in height, and known as the Sechelt Image.

Several considerations, however, combine to suggest that the story of personal tragedy may be too recent an origin, and too simple an explanation for this work of art.

The Sechelt say that their ancestors maintained a garrison on SKWAH'-LAHWT, Thormanby Island, during aboriginal times. During their tours of duty at this outpost, young warriors, the cream of the aristocracy, were entrusted with both sentry duty and the manning of the fort, KUHL'-AH-KHAN, located on the western shore of the island. KAY'-KAH-LAH-KUHM, the boy's home village, was so named because a palisade was maintained there.

Following established tradition, raiders of old would have appeared at this post or at another similar post, to engage in a skirmish with young men of the garrison. The typical Salish palisade was built with sufficient space between each post for use of a lance, TCHAY'-KOH-NATCH, as a weapon. Since the lance was thrust rather than thrown, its range was limited. Both attackers and defenders could avoid serious injury. In any case, the event was pre-arranged. An attack would constitute an element not of warfare but of ceremony. While customs established centuries ago prevailed, it is unlikely that a renegade band could have eluded watchers along the coast to as far south as the locale of this story.

When such unauthorized gangs did maraud these shores, early in the nineteenth century, the making of stone sculptures had already waned. If the story is true, it could have been set very long ago, at a time before boundaries between peoples became established and accepted.

Complications also arise from the work of stone itself. While the body exhibits female characteristics, the object referred to in the tragic story as the figure of a child also resembles a phallus.[8] Facial features, referred to by the Sechelt as MUH-OHSS'-TUHN, bear little resemblance to either female or male members of this people at any time since their likenesses were recorded by foreign visitors.

Clarence Joe said that, whatever its origin or its purpose, the Sechelt Image is very, very old.

Chapter Eleven

Not all healing was directed at the soul. Bodily ailments also afflicted these people. Within their homeland, they found plants which served not only as foods, but also as medicines against these afflictions.

Most elderly Sechelt apparently knew the medicines provided by nature. Older women, so it is said, used to follow TCHIHT'-WIHN, the black bear, after it came out of hibernation in the springtime. The bear's first search was for a tonic, to cleanse its system after long months without nourishment. Whatever TCHIHT'-WIHN dug up to eat, the women would dig for their people who, though they had not hibernated, had spent winter months eating mostly dried and smoked fish, clams, and meats. As the bear went from one plant to another, the women added each to their list of tonics and general medicines. While women knew most about natural medicines, men also knew many of the plants and shrubs that could be used.

During one brief afternoon's outing, Basil Joe found some thirty plants and shrubs that had been used by his people, within a stone's throw of public roadways near Sechelt. About half of these were medicines. Basil also alluded to many other shrubs, plants, and vines, which grew only on mountain slopes or in certain inlet valleys.

When Mrs. Ellen Paull and Mrs. Mary Jeffery saw the samples gathered on this expedition, they gave the same name to each specimen as Basil Joe had designated, and indicated precisely the same food or medicinal use for each. They also alluded to the many other leaves, roots, flowers, berries, and vines which they themselves had once gathered during summer seasons.

As may be well imagined, a number of these remedies pertained to wounds and bone fractures. Basil Joe spoke many times of a patch of low plants effective in the treatment of wounds and infections. He recalled the existence of such a patch – one of the only patches he knew to exist locally – at Wilson Creek, TSAH'-KWOHM, and found it quite readily, even though he had not visited the spot for many years. This plant, the wild ginger, he referred to as HUHT-HUHT-TAHN'. The leaf, crushed was applied to a wound to speed healing. The aromatic leaves were also placed in food-storage lodges to counteract the sometimes not-too-pleasant odors emanating from smoked and dried fish, cockles, and meat that had been hung there during many months. It was too powerful a medicine to be taken internally, Basil said.

Elmer McDannald, who logged with Basil Joe in Deserted Valley, testified to the healing powers of this plant. An axe cut laid his left thumb open from end to end. Apparently a patch of HUHT-HUHT-TAHN' was growing nearby, for Elmer said that Basil very quickly had some leaves ready, which he applied to the wound with the prognosis that it would be healed within three days' time. In three days the wound did heal, said Elmer, leaving only a hairline scar.

Some of the HUHT-HUHT-TAHN' leaves which I gathered in the company of Basil Joe and his son Ben were put to immediate use. The nail of one of my toes had been wrenched off and the toe had become badly inflamed. I applied some of these medicinal leaves to the injury. Eight hours later, swelling and pain were reduced and healing had commenced.

KWAH'-LAY-WAHN, Western maianthemun, is similar in size and shape to wild ginger but lighter in colour and smoother in texture. While not as powerful as the other plant, this was also used extensively by the Sechelt people. It still grows quite plentifully in the woods today.

A third natural healer, KWIHN'-ASTH, referred to in botany texts as Indian hellebore, was found high up mountain valleys. According to accounts from a number of Sechelt, it was gathered for use each summer well into the twentieth century. The healing ingredients of this plant are located in its roots. Dried, the root is so hard that a file or sharp rock must be used to remove particles, which are then used to make a solution. Applied to a wound, this remedy, so it is said, not only healed but also deadened pain. The Sechelt say that it is, like HUHT-HUHT-TAHN', too strong to be swallowed.

If an injury results in severe bleeding, stanching the flow of blood is of more immediate concern than healing. The Sechelt treated such injuries with a brew made from the root of the ironwood shrub, KAH'-LAH-KYE.

Where there were extensive wounds, the women would gather bark from the wild plum, TUHL-SUHLSS', chew it to make it soft, and apply it to the injury. This was one of the medicines used, according to the traditional story, when the young brother was clawed by MY'-OOK, the grizzly, up in the valley of TSOH'-NYE. Gum from the cherry tree, KWUHT-NAY'-TSEYE, was also used in the treatment of wounds.

If a poultice was needed, an application was made of cooked leaves of the plantain, HOH-HAHM-SLAY'-WYE, a plant so named because the frog, HOH'-HAHM, would sit on its smooth, flat surface. Flowers of the yarrow, WAH'-OHSS-KLETCH, found growing in dry sandy soil near the beach, were also used as a poultice.

The soft, feathery leaves of this plant also possessed medicinal properties. A brew from these leaves, alone or mixed with fat to form a lotion, could be applied to irritated skin. Roots of the yarrow were chewed to clean teeth and to keep them hard.

A solution made from the roots of OHT'-SKYE, the snowberry, was used to promote the mending of bones. Mrs. Ellen Paull said that an aunt of hers once had both legs broken near the ankles when a shed collapsed on her. The woman spent several months in a Vancouver hospital, said Mrs. Paull, but the bones would not knit. Finally, she returned home. Each day her people immersed her lower limbs in a solution made from boiled roots of the OHT'-SKYE. Within two months, so Mrs. Paull said, the aunt could walk again. Berries from this shrub were squeezed against warts to remove them.

Certain plants provided general tonics. Best known among these, used by early European settlers and by Chinese herbalists still today, was SAL'-IH-BOY, a shrub known as Hudson's Bay tea. This shrub grows around the marshy margins of lakes in this area. Tender shoots of the salmonberry, SWAY'-KAHL, known to many European settlers by its Chinook name, MUHK'-AH-MUHK, also provided a popular tonic in spring.

During winter months, to offset overly rich dried fish and meats, the Sechelt occasionally drew on their supplies of KUH'-OH-PYE, the wild crabapple. They kept the crabapples stored in holes dug beside streams near their villages, where cold water could circulate. The holes were lined with leaves of the thimbleberry, TOH'-KWOHM. Partially cooked, this apple formed a sauce, called KUH-OH-PYE'-OH-TSAIN, that was both medicinal and tasty.

The earliest spring tonic, for which the Sechelt competed with TCHIHT'-WIHN, the black bear, was the tuber root of what is now commonly called the skunk cabbage, HOH-HOH-KWAHM'. During early summer, fruits of the salmonberry, SKWAY'-KOH-LYE, and of the thimbleberry, TOH'-KWOHM, added both to taste and tonic in the everyday diet.

The wild blackberry, TCH-TOO'-KIHN; the huckleberry, SKOO-LOH'-MAH; and the mountain blueberry, HUH-MAHTH'-NATCH, were needed in such great quantities that women travelled far up inlet valleys in search of them. These berries were prepared for winter use, when hot, sunny days permitted, by a process the Sechelt called TAHK'-AH. Berries of the TCH-TOO'-KIHN, the SKOO-LOH'-MAH, and the HUH-MAHTH'-NATCH were smashed against a board placed to face the sun. Excess juice was caught in a bowl and ladled slowly over the pulp. The TAHK'-AH, carried on by a woman too elderly to climb hillsides in search of the berries, was continued until all juice was dried into the berry pulp. Then the paste was wrapped in thimbleberry leaves, which would not affect the taste, for winter storage.

Quantities of bearberry, when beaten into a froth in a new cooking-basket, kept the basket permanently sweet thereafter. The bearberry, KAH-AH'-NYE, was known far and wide by its Chinook name, SOHP'-AH-LAH-LEE.

A mixture of KAH-AH'-NYE, the bearberry; STAY'-KAH, the salal berry; and MUHM-TSEYE', the wild current, when beaten together made SHWOH'-SHOHM — literally, "Indian ice-cream." This was a delicacy as well as a necessary part of the aboriginal diet.

Elderberries, TCHAY'-OH-KYE, were preserved in jelly form.

Wild pepper, TSAH'-OOTCH; Indian pipe, HOH'-ATSK; and wild rhubarb, YAH-LAH'-UHP, were usually gathered to be cooked with meat, clams, or fish, as seasoning. Throughout the year, women strove to maintain a tonic element in their foods.

A number of plants and shrubs provided specific remedies.

Considering the wet environment in which they lived, native coastal Indians were remarkably free from the ravages of rheumatism and arthritis. They attributed this to a tea made from the roots of the devil's club, TCHAH-AH'-TYE. The same brew was apparently used, along with other ingredients, as a curative for tuberculosis, one of the most disastrous of the diseases acquired from Europeans. Elderly Sechelt, during the early 1960s, told of many individuals, white as well as Indian, who had been cured through persistent taking of this medicine.

Smallpox, most devastating of all diseases brought to these shores aboard early sailing and steam vessels, was combated by a treatment which itself inflicted terrible suffering upon the patient. In spite of severe fever usually brought on by the disease, the patient was almost roasted before an open fire. At the same time, he was obliged to swallow great quantities of hot sea water, while oil of the ratfish, SKOO'-NAH, was rubbed into his chest and back.

For colds, the Sechelt learned to make a tea from the meaty roots of the licorice fern, STEW'-AHK, and from the fiddles of the sword fern, SAUGH-AH-LAY'-AHM.

To stop diarrhea, they ate wild strawberries, TIHL'-AH-KAHK.

The cascara, still used as a base for tonic medicines, was well known to the aboriginal Sechelt. Bark from this tree, HUHM'-EYE, was stripped off carefully so as to leave an inner layer for regrowth. Basil Joe said that well into his lifetime, containers of a brew made from bits of this bark were kept on stoves in homes of elder Sechelt people, to be sipped each day, despite its bitter taste.

To keep the heart in good condition, the Sechelt ate seed hips of the wild rose, KUII-WIIUHN'-EYE.

As has already been mentioned, water from HUHK-AHLS-SAY'-KO, "The Spring of the Gods," off Smuggler's Cove, was considered medicinal. Basil Joe brought a container of water back to Sechelt on his return home from a trip to this spring in 1962. Mrs. Mary Jeffery maintained that a severe inflammation of his eyes was eased after bathing them in this water.

One of the most fascinating uses of a potion made from natural plants was that of endowing one who drank it with great strength and enduring stamina. Basil Joe, late in his life, recalled having partaken of such a concoction as a young man. At the time, his generation was participating in canoe racing, once very popular with the Sechelt. His grandmother, so he said, would prepare him for a competition with a brew she had made for the occasion. The administration of this drink took place, Basil recalled, once daily for three days.

On each of the first two days, he became numb, TCHIHL-KAHT'-AHN, and fell asleep. When he awakened, he threw up quite violently. On the third day, the potion so elated him that his feet seemed to move without touching the ground when he ran. He was tireless at paddling a racing canoe. He felt as though he could run up a mountain; and on one occasion, fortified with his grandmother's preparation, he did run to the top of KULSE, his people's sacred mountain, which rises 7,500 feet above the site of the former village of HUHN'-AH-TCHIN at the head of Jervis Inlet.

But, said Basil, he had never managed to watch his grandmother make this brew. He thought that he knew some of the ingredients; but he was certain that he did not know all of them. There were either five or seven in all, he believed. Nor did he at any time know the proportion of each root used. Later in life, so Basil said, he had wished for the knowledge of this amazing drink; but he had never brought himself to experiment with a potion lest he concoct something harmful rather than helpful.[1]

Many other medicines existed. As already mentioned, some are no longer encountered because the people no longer ascend mountain valleys each summer to gather the ingredients. Some have been abandoned to modern medicines and treatments. Others, particularly those in the realm of the healer, were never thoroughly understood by the populace.

Basil told of a flower whose Sechelt name, SPAH'-NAHK, could be translated to mean "Pink Stranger." It was a small flower on a small plant, said Basil. Possibly this was a star flower, or one called Indian potato, but its exact identity cannot be confirmed now. According to Basil, a person could use this flower to attract affection from one of the other sex. Shakespeare, in *A Midsummer Night's Dream*[2] has Oberon say:

> Yet mark'd I where the bolt of Cupid fell.
> It fell upon a little western flower,
> Before milk-white, now purple with love's wound,
> And maidens call it love-in-idleness.
> Fetch me that flower, the herb I shew'd thee once.
> The juice of it on sleeping eye-lids laid
> Will make or man or woman madly dote
> Upon the next live creature that it sees.[3]

Shakespeare's love-in-idleness was the wild pansy, the violet, but its equivalent is not known here. It is doubtful that Basil's SPAH'-NAHK is a violet; Basil would have known the violet.

Another love plant was the AY-YAHL'-AY-WAH, a low gray-leafed trailing plant, the leaves of which are soapy when rubbed together. This is the plant referred to later as that which induced the medicine man's vision. Basil said that a young woman in Deserted Bay once washed her hair in water in which she had soaked some leaves of this plant. Her sweetheart in Vancouver Bay, scorning his canoe, ran over the intervening mountains to her.

Traditional Indian medicines give rise to puzzles, answers to which must sometimes be sought beyond the province of natural phenomena.

The earliest European explorers and traders found the peoples of the Pacific Northwest free from Europe's diseases, particularly smallpox and tuberculosis. This might be explained on the grounds that such diseases never existed in this region of the world. No doubt, microbes specific to these, or to many other common Eurasian diseases, never developed here. Conditions in cities of those continents which gave rise to some of these diseases were rather appalling. Such conditions did not prevail along the north Pacific Coast.

There is of course another possibility, less palatable to the pragmatic, scientific Western mind, but one that must be reckoned with, nevertheless. An argument to the effect that no human being could attain spiritual power from the sun or from some physically superior entity, or could make use of this power, might be accepted widely; but such acceptance does not guarantee its truth. The Western world has held spiritual power suspect of forces of darkness since ancient times.

North American aborigines, while acknowledging the existence of evil spirits as well as of good, quite readily distinguished one from the other, and never doubted that the EYE'-SEE-AY-AHK used his powers for good. Nor did they doubt that these powers were supernatural and able to conquer the forces of evil. Well, sickness is evil; germs are evil. Physical forces, in the forms of medicines, were employed to combat diseases; and spiritual forces were also invoked.

Because Western minds understand the one and not the other, they tend to accept substantial physical properties, and to reject insubstantial spiritual forces, even while giving lip service to such cliches as "mind over matter," and despite the fact that they think that they comprehend psychosomatic interrelationships.

If human scientists cannot entirely accept, as explanations of the absence of virulent diseases among such peoples as the Sechelt, the hypothesis that the EYE'-SEE-AY-UHK, who derived his power from the sun and who worked for good, successfully combated such derivations of evil, surely they can at least keep open minds and admit the possibility of such an explanation. In this story, this explanation will be found acceptable.

Chapter Twelve

The opinion has often been voiced that time was literally ignored in the aboriginal North American way of life. This opinion is based on the Occidental concept that time varies directly in importance with the quantity of goods produced during each of its intervals. This thinking, however, cannot be applied to the North American aboriginal ethos. Here it was realized that time, far from acting as an impediment to production, was an essential ingredient in the creation of works. An appropriate quantity of time as well as effort was needed to produce something worthy of taking its place among its predecessors.

Western civilizations have come to look upon time as a phenomenon that flows past and is gone. "Tempus fugit," or "Time flies" is an expression known to all who live by a dated calendar. Time is a river, according to Western culture; each of us floats in a private scallop on its current towards the sea of infinity. The past is a very real but irretrievable section of this stream behind us; the future, a very real but invisible course ahead.

In quite marked contrast to this concept, time to the aboriginal mind was all that had ever happened. Each new moment was merely added to this immensity.[1] Time was more like a lake than a river. All existed, not in a state of flux, but rather held in a kind of suspension. What we think of today as the future could be peered into, and has been within recent years, by Native Indians still able to visualize time and space as their forefathers understood these concepts.[2]

Tom MacInnes,[3] writing of the Chinook jargon, commented on this aboriginal concept of time, and its close similarity to the manner in which time was regarded in the Orient:

> Long ago, and alone under a pine tree on a hilltop, an Indian came and told things to me between sound and silence that were taboo (distant in spiritual time). When leaving, he gave an all-round wave of his arm, and said "Kwonsum Sokalie Tyhee Mamook kopa sokalie. Pe kwonsum Yo mitlite Yo." That is to say, "Forever the Lord on High worketh, But forever Yo stays Yo."
>
> How about that? How about the notion of Yo, the eternal, unexistent yet potential matrix; anterior to God as the sky is anterior to the sun?
>
> I remember how that unusual talk with that unusual Indian came back to me many years after, in Dr. George Morrison's library at Pekin. I was beginning a rare version of the Scripture of the Heavenly Way. Those characters were turned into words for me: "Dau do kau foy chwang dau."–"The doing that can be done is not the regular doing!" And that is only another way of saying what the Indian had said to me on the hilltop under the pine tree when I was a boy: "The Divine that can be divined is not the Eternal Divine!"[4]

Like most ancient peoples, the Sechelt perceived that cycles in natural phenomena on earth corresponded to movements and positions of heavenly bodies.

The sun, SEE-AY'-UHK, was seen as the source of all life. The same term, SEE-AY'-UHK, applied to the medicine man, indicating the belief that this personage derived his power from the giver of all power, the sun. The artist-medicine man who left the insignia of the circle within the cave mouth as SHAK'-KWOHT proved, by so doing, that power derived from the sun could conquer that inherent in any earthly phenomenon. In this instance, the phenomenon involved the life-destroying vapours that appeared when lightning struck this spot.

The Sechelt understood and made use of such concepts as the year, the month, and, of course, the day. They saw the year, SKOH'-MYE,[5] as a grand cycle; but they did not number each in sequence as civilizations of Europe came to do.

Within the annual cycle, there were a fixed series of lesser cycles, each demarked by the life and death of SHEHL'-SHEHL, the moon. Today, many Westerners have a feeling of superior bemusement toward such an expression as "many moons ago" as the idiom of a slightly lesser culture. This attitude persists despite the fact that European civilizations somewhat inaccurately designated their twelve divisions of the year as months; that is, as "moonths."

Each of the life-spans of SHEHL'-SHEHL, the Sechelt noted, was accompanied by some natural phenomenon. During its first cycle, for instance – known now as January – SKWEET-OOL', the raven, laid its eggs. This first moon of the year thus became known as SKWEET-OOL'-SHEHL'-SHEHL; literally, "Raven Month."

February, the month during which LAY'-AHM, the long-necked loon, laid its eggs, was known as LAY'-AHM-SHEHL'-SHEHL. March, when the black cod, KWOHM'-KWOHM, laid its eggs was KWOHM-KWOHM-SHEHL-SHEHL. April, when cod eggs began to hatch was hatching moon, NUHM'-SHEHL'-SHEHL. May, when the salmonberry, KWAIL'-KWOHL, began to grow was SAH'-ATCH-KYE-KWAIL'-KWOHL-SHEHL'-SHEHL. June, when the salmonberries ripened, was ripening month, SAH'-ATCH-KYE-SHEHL'-SHEHL. July, when HUHN'-OHN, the humpback salmon, first arrived was HUHN'-OHN-SHEHL-SHEHL. August, when TAHK'-AH, the drying of berries took place was TAHK'-AH-SHEHL'-SHEHL. September, during which HUHN'-OHN began to enter streams was TUHM-HUHN'-OHN-SHEHL'-SHEHL. October, moon of YAH'-NOH-KWUH, the dog-salmon was YAH'-NOH KWUII-SHEHL'-SHEHL. November, during which KUHM-EYE'-AT, the coho, spawned was KUHM-EYE'-AT-SHEHL'-SHEHL. In December, for the first time, skin would come off summer-smoked salmon when cooked. This month was NUHM'-SHEHL'-SHEHL, the same designation as for April. This was because the skin of the cooked salmon shed much as cod-egg coverings as they hatched.

The foregoing names, while accurate to a certain extent, do not correspond exactly to our present-day calendar months. Since the moon takes between twenty-nine and thirty days to complete a cycle, twelve cycles fall approximately ten days short of a solar year.[6] Basil Joe said that his people simply did not count these days. The interval coincided almost exactly with our present-day Christmas holidays. The first moon-cycle, SKWEET-OOL'-SHEHL'-SHEHL, was then begun at the beginning of the new solar cycle, SKOH'-MYE.

Early Sechelt recognized the same phases of the moon as the ones recognized today. The new moon they called HAH'-WAHSS-

SHEHL'-SHEHL; the quarters, SUHK'-SHEHL'-SHEHL; and the full moon, STUH-LAITCH'-SHEHL'-SHEHL; that is "round moon." Changes in the moon's shape were caused by PUHK'-UHL, the Barrows gold-eye duck, who, they said, nested on the moon. Since the word PUHK is a Sechelt term for our word "soul," then it was probably the spiritual Gold-Eye, the Gold-Eye of mythology, who brought about the moon's phases.[7]

Within each moon-cycle, the Sechelt gave names to each day, the seven divisions of each quarter. Jennie Erickson, whose memory was filled with detailed Sechelt terminology, said that Thursday was known as SMOHSS. Since the aboriginal word MOHSS indicated the number four, it is possible that the Sechelt traditionally began their week with Monday, which they called YEE-LAH-WAHSS'-EE-EHS. Tuesday was SAHM-EE'-EHS; Wednesday, SCHAIN-AHW'-EE-EHS; Friday, TSKAL'-AY-TCHAY'-EHS; Saturday, TSUHK-WAHT'-AHM; and Sunday, TSKAH-HAHT'-EHN-AT.[8]

The Sechelt also devised a means for telling time during daylight hours, but this knowledge is now lost. Likely, it was based on either the position of the sun in the sky, or on rise and fall of the tides.

As these people were dependent on tides for travel and for food gathering, they observed the tides very closely. They discovered that their ebbs and flows corresponded in time with the moon's positions, and in extent with its phases. High tide they called KUHM'-MAY-UHL; low tide, TCHOOK-SAY'-WOHSS, and strong tide, TSEYE-AHM'-KOH. The extreme low tide that occurs once a year during August was TUH-KAH-MAH-LAY'-KOH.

The star, KOH'-SUHN, freely interpreted as "powerful sun," also played its part in Sechelt reckoning. Long ages past, these people realized that both direction and time could be determined from a cluster of stars in the northern heavens, TSOH'-KWUH. One group of stars which swung slowly about one fixed star resembled a cooking utensil. They called the constellation SOHP-AN-ATCH-KWAH'-KWOH-WIHSS, "a pot with a handle," our Big Dipper. The fixed star, our Polaris, could be used as a bearing point. By close observation of the Dipper, they learned what time of night it indicated at any given position in TSOH'-KWUH, the sky, during varying seasons of the year. Positions of certain other stars also helped to fix seasons.

Two other constellations were given names by the Sechelt. One was seen as STUHM-TOH'-MISH, the Archer, with his bow drawn. The other was his quarry, MY'-OOK, the Grizzly Bear. In Sechelt

Inlet, about one-half mile up inlet from the western entrance to Salmon Arm, two life-size figures, in pure white quartz, stand out against the granite. One is known as STUHM-TOH'-MISH, the Bowman. He stands in a position to shoot. A giant arrow is aimed at MY'-OOK, the Grizzly, who is reared for a charge. Since the bow is held in a horizontal position, it does not show in this natural sculpture. Whether or not the rock tableau suggested the constellation's name makes interesting speculation. In any case, both stone and star have intrigued the Sechelt people through untold centuries.

Positions of SEE-AY'-UHK, the Sun, were also given names far back in time. Sunrise was called KWUHT-EYE'-NAH-TAH-SEE-AY'-UHK; a good occasion, since winter nights were long and dark. Noon was called KWUH-OH'-TAH-SEE-AY'-UHK;[9] and the sunset, when the sun seems to be closing its eye, UH'-UHM-TAH-SEE-AY'-UHK.

All of these reckonings can be more or less logically accounted for by scrupulous and intricate observations. These observations were retained and worked over until forced to yield systems by which seasons, time, tide, and direction could be determined. The uninitiated must realize, however, that although a particular system was evolved, each reckoner was obliged to perform his own observations—of moon phase, of sun and star position, or of whatever natural phenomenon or combination of phenomena his immediate reckoning required.

Other computations are not so readily explained. For instance, Basil Joe's skill in determining the tide's time and height along the Strait of Georgia coast and into Jervis Inlet can be, as has been suggested, attributed to both lore handed down to him from his predecessors and his own keen sense of observation. His ability to reckon the ebbs and flows and the slack water times of KLAY'-KO, the Sechelt Rapids, is not so easily accounted for. This is particularly true during certain spring tides, when such a vast quantity of water[10] accumulates that only three tidal changes take place, rather than the regular four.

Basil could give accurate times to slack water during such occurrences form Sechelt villages twenty-five miles away. He could make accurate computations even when official tide tables were wrong. On at least one occasion, he showed that the computation of TUH-KUH-MAH-LAY'-KO, the lowest annual tide, erred by three days, driving stakes into the low water mark on successive days to prove his point. Even more baffling was his ability to predict a slack in the dangerous Yaculta Rapids when, again, the time given in the book of tables was inaccurate. Published tide tables are, of course, based on information recorded through exhaustive surveys; and they are essentially accurate. The point is that, on the rare occasion that some unpredictable factor altered the predicted slack water time, Basil could sense this before he had committed his craft to the currents of one of our powerful coastal rapids.

And when, nearing eighty years of age, Basil Joe retired after thirty-five seasons of skippering seineboats, throughout the length of British Columbia's coastline, he did so without having ever scraped a keel on an uncharted reef. This record, which was worthy of comment at a dinner held to commemorate Basil's retirement, was attained without benefit of radar or other sophisticated navigation equipment.

Reg Paull, while logging at the head of Narrows Arm, the Sechelt's KLYE'-EH-KWIHM, would make the run to Porpoise Bay in the camp speedboat in the evening, gather and load supplies, and set out for camp again, thirty miles away, under a sky black with cloud, at midnight or later. There was neither beacon nor light of any other kind to guide a mariner, and the open boat carried neither spotlight nor compass. Reg tried to explain the sense by which he knew not only the channel, which closes to within one hundred yards at KO'-KAH, Narrows Arm Rapids, but also the presence of tide rips, for which he had to slow his speed in case of driftwood.

Obviously, all attempts at explanation fail. But the trips continued, over a course that no qualified master mariner would care to follow without all of the instruments of his art. He might admit, though, having occasionally been guided by the same inexplicable forces that guided Reg Paull.

Chapter Thirteen

One of the most widespread mysteries left from primitive cultures involves pictographs, more commonly known as rock paintings. Examples are found in every continent. Painted rock carvings in Tibet, at the roof of the world in Asia, are considered sacred and are visited by pilgrims. Africa, near the Sahara region, and Australia, particularly northern Queensland, abound in pictograph galleries. Best known examples in Europe are those discovered in the caves of Altamira in Spain. Since their discovery by modern cultures, uncounted thousands of these pictures, executed on ceilings and walls of caves or on protected cliff faces, have come to light. North America has its share of these paintings from the past. A broad belt of pictographs extends from coast to coast in Canada. In 1968, John Corner of Vernon published *Pictographs in the Interior of British Columbia*[1] which included the results of many years of his studies on this topic. The coast of the province, particularly from Howe Sound to Bella Coola, reveals a prodigiously long line of panels. Of this tremendous array of natural easels, the shorelines of Jervis and Sechelt inlets reveal – and conceal – some of the clearest paintings of all.

Whether realistic or stylistic, these paintings represent some of the least understood relics of bygone cultures. Thousands of paintings have been copied. Hundreds of articles have been written on their artistry and their possible origins. Any true history of when they were painted, who painted them, or of what function they were meant to perform remains unknown.

111

Throughout the Pacific Northwest, petroglyphs – scratchings on rock – are comparatively well known. Many of these depict a creature, or the face of a creature, outlined by shallow grooves scored into flat rock surfaces. Many figures are rather crude and inartistic by standards of European art, and seem devoid of meaning deeper than whatever may have been meant to be conveyed through their direct pictorial representations. Some, particularly those in Petroglyph Park a few miles south of Nanaimo, are apparently quite old. Others, so some scientists maintain, probably date back no farther than two hundred years. The best known and the most artistic carvings are found in the Bella Coola Valley.

Sites of most pictographs are known to very few persons. There are, for instance, about twenty pictographs or panels of pictographs still in existence today scattered throughout Jervis and Sechelt inlets. Some murals contain as many as a dozen symbols. All are red in colour, done in mercuric sulfide, commonly known as cinnabar; and known as TUHM'-UHLTH by the Sechelt people. There is little doubt that these paintings date back some distance in time.[2] Some have existed without perceptible change since white settlers and loggers first began to make their way about these inlets.

Pictographs executed on surfaces protected from weathering by overhanging ledges are still perfectly clear today – a deep, rich red. Possibly through the action of their mercuric content, these paintings have penetrated into the granite rock on which they were drawn. No particle of the paint can be flaked off for examination. It can be removed only by chipping away the rock itself. In 1973, a local fisherman chopped into a shapeless blot of paint in the Bella Bella area, and found that the red coloration penetrated two inches into the rock.

Here in traditional inlets, a veil of mystery has shrouded these relics up to the present day. Even among those who know something of their histories, revelation of the pictographs' secrets does not come easily.

In the first place, the questioner does not usually know what questions to ask. As with all research, the questioner must know something of his subject before he can ask an intelligent question.

Since no written source exists, information of this sort can be gained only from direct human contact. Over time, the questioner will find that the sort of information he is receiving is gradually changing. If he understands anything of primitive lore, he will realize that he is being told information of a progressively more secret nature.

One reason for the secrecy regarding Sechelt rock paintings is that they were painted by their SEE-AY'-UHK, their medicine man. Native persons themselves thus know little of their ancestral pictographs. The entire story of any one painting is not known; and never was known by the people in general.Some of the symbolism has survived, however, as have some of the stories behind it. Something of the general history of these relics can be pieced together. Basil Joe, in talks over a period of several years, removed some of the veils that have obscured the meanings of these Indian rock paintings.

The best known story depicted is that of the hunter pulled overboard by a porpoise he had harpooned. This painting, about seven miles up Sechelt Inlet from the head of Porpoise Bay, shows a full-faced view of what is said to be TCHAIN'-KO, the Sea-Serpent, god of the waters. According to the legend, when people came by after the tragedy, they noticed a scar running up the mountainside, freshly gouged into the rock itself. Since only TCHAIN'-KO, who could pass clear through a mountain, could have left such a mark, they reasoned that he must have been involved in the strange event. Just how the Serpent was involved in the drowning, however, and in the journey of the fisherman's soul to the porpoise kingdom remains a mystery.[2]

Conversely, although nothing is known of the story behind the painting just below Earl's Cove, at SKUH-HUHL', something is known of how it came to be placed there. Following whatever incident provoked need for a painting, the SEE-AY'-UHK responsible was obliged to go in his canoe to NAH'-PATH, about a mile inside Princess Louisa Inlet, SWAY-WE'-LAHT. There, so the account runs, he slept in his canoe. In his sleep, a vision came to him, induced by a herb he had rubbed on his forehead. What he saw in his vision he later painted on the rock face as SKUH-HUHL'.[3]

About three miles toward the head of Jervis Inlet from Malibu Rapids, the largest panel in this inlet appears on the wall of a niche in the side of an enormous boulder. A heavily outlined circle dominates the centre of a mural some twenty feet in length. Other prominent figures show three killer whales, STAH'-LAH-SHAN, guiding the Serpent, TCHAIN'-KO, and a distinct outline of a human eye.[4] The paintings appear to have been limned with very thick paint—perhaps many layers of paint as years went by. The floor of the niche shows signs of fire. Near the wall are piles of smooth stones of approximately fist-size. Some retain faint signs of having been marked in places with red paint.[5]

According to myth of ancient India, life appeared from the cosmic egg of Narayana, the Divine Creator,[6] portrayed as a seven-headed serpent. Through a fascinating succession of names, this symbolism travelled through ancient Babylonia and Greece and arrived at Eastre, the Teutonic Goddess of Spring, who for may years has been commemorated by the Easter egg. Across the same area, to the western extremities of Europe in Portugal, through Wales, and even as far north as Scandinavia, smooth stones flecked with paint have been found in caves, as if whatever peoples daubed them sought to imitate the markings of eggs.[7] The term "soul stones" has been used, on occasion, to designate these paint-marked smooth bits of rock.[8]

No other writings about archaeological finds in North America seem to have mentioned relics of this sort. Yet they are here on the Pacific shores of this continent, half a globe away from their likenesses to east and to west. When questioned on the subject, Reg Paull said that in aboriginal times, his people ate no eggs except, ritually, those of the sea gull, KWAH-KWAY'.[9] According to Sechelt myth, said Reg, all was dark when the world was new. One day Mink, KYE'-AHKS, heard a voice calling her. It was Sea Gull, who was in a closed box with a thorn in his foot. Mink, finding that she could not help with the lid closed, flipped it off. Out streamed a radiance from the shining KWAH-KWAY', who then placed SEE-AY'-UHK, the Sun, in the sky to give light.[10] The sea gull was thus a sacred bird to the ancient Sechelt, to be respected and not be harmed. The sun is sometimes referred to as KWAH-KWAY' in the Sechelt language in reference to the myth that Sea Gull created it.

Reg said that eggs were generally used only in the AY-YIHM'-UHSS, the spirit power dance. Those to be used were punctured and blown, and their shells were strung around the staff held by the dancer. Although he was frequently carried away by ecstasy, and even though he fell unconscious at the end of his ritual, the dancer was forbidden to break any of his eggs, represented by their shells.[12]

Whether or not the niche, near the head of Jervis Inlet, constituted the site of a ceremony cannot be determined now. However, Basil Joe did say that it was once one of his people's most significant "secret" places.

Almost all paintings include a circle somewhere in the composite of symbols. Since the painter, the medicine man, drew his power from the sun—the term SEE-AY'-UHK designating both sun and medicine man—it is quite likely that this circle denoted his sign—also the sign of esoteric initiation.

A short distance up Jervis Inlet from the mouth of Osgood Creek, a boulder sits amid foliage several yards in from the solid rock shore. From under one curved side of this granite stone, a beautifully executed likeness of a Hebrew Menorah emerges, red in colour and between two and three feet in width and height. As in the Menorah, the stems are thick and their tops flanged as if to receive candles. An interchange of candle socket and cobra head would emphasize the remarkable similarities exhibited by the candelabrum with its seven branches and the Narayana, the "Seven Intellects" of ancient India, from which all life was said to have come.[12a] One cannot view the seven-stemmed figure painted on the Jervis Inlet boulder without speculating on the ageless "Tree of Life," so fundamental to the mythologies of many peoples across much of the earth.

Among the rock paintings, a ladder is sometimes depicted. The large panel that survives near the foot of Sakinaw Lake contains such a figure of almost actual size—an observer feels almost like endeavoring to scale the cliff on which it is painted by means of its natural-looking rungs. It is possible that the ladder symbol is concerned with a legend. According to one such story, a man once heard a TCHAY'-TAY-LAITCH, the Sechelt's symbol for good fortune, crying from the cliff at this spot. The man could not reach it, however, and was therefore doomed to bad luck. Another possibility is that the ladder symbol is purely mythological and unrelated to anything physical.

To the right of this ladderlike painting, a fish[13] is depicted, about the size and shape of a sea bass. To the right again, a row of symbols appears one above the other. The lowest of these appears between only two and three feet above the present-day level of the lake. A circle, the likeness of a crayfish, and a beautifully-outlined turtle constitute prominent symbols in this tableau. The painted turtle is still to be found in both Ruby Lake, SAH'-LATH, and Sakinaw Lake, SAUGH'-AH-NAH. To the Sechelt, SAUGH'-AH-NAH "belonged" to KAY-KAH'-LAH, the Turtle. He could literally say of it, "TOH'-TOH-LAH." He was "The Man of the Lake"; he knew everything about this significant body of near-tidal water.[14] An almost invisible portrayal of TCHAIN'-KO, his head uppermost, half encloses the other symbols.[15]

The human semblance, with round head and sticklike arms and legs outspread, appears in two paintings; one at Earl's Cove and one between Osgood and Sechal creeks, halfway up Jervis Inlet. As usual, almost nothing is known about these symbols. In other parts of the northwestern Pacific Coast, however, carved wooden figures with enlarged heads and shrunken bodies, as in these paintings, have been found at burial sites. Apparently they were "guardians" over those buried there. The pictograph at Earl's Cove is faded. The painting farther up inlet is sharp and clear, however, at the back of a tiny niche some fifteen feet above sea level. It is entirely possible that these symbols stand guard over now-nameless dead who perished at or near their posts.

Near the head of Salmon Arm, about one-half mile above the bay at Misery Creek, the Sechelt's WISH-IHM'-SHIHN, a sheer cliff rises at right angles to the shoreline. Near the base of this cliff where a natural stone ramp leads up from the water across it, several figures appear quite sharply. One is the treelike symbol already referred to. Near it, placed so that a natural green coloration in the stone acts as a nose, a monster's face peers out. Beyond it again, to the left and farther up the ramp, a solidly-coloured double-headed TCHAIN'-KO is depicted, the two heads facing each other. Even the most cursory glance reveals that these are not the features of ordinary serpents. Ears protrude above the heads and the jaws are extended to create profiles more like those of horses than of snakes. The shortened bodies curve to left and right from a common point. Stylized lines give the appearance of very large scales. A representation of the prow of a Viking Dragon Ship of a thousand years ago fits the head and neck portions of one of these figures almost exactly, even to the simulated scale markings. The ancient Chinese Dragon, though somewhat more ornate, was of basically the same appearance. A stylized mountain goat, SWAYT'-LYE, with hoofs elongated to look much like feet, appears between the two heads of the Serpent. To the left again, two deer appear in solid colour. Above them is a symbol like a widely opened "U."

Reg Paull, master of much of his people's esoteric lore, said that, although the two bodies are not interwound, this portrayal of TCHAIN'-KO is meant to represent the "Twined" or "Twinned" Serpent. In this form, Reg explained, TCHAIN'-KO is not destructive, but protective. Here he is shown supporting the life of the human being, symbolized by the stylized goat. In all, said Reg, the figure is meant to convey much the same idea as does the Caduceus, the twined serpents of Hermes, symbol of the medical profession today.

On the eastern shore of Agamemnon Channel, LEAL'-KO-

MAIN, about three miles up from the mouth of Sakinaw Creek, a tiny cave is located about fifteen feet above sea level in the middle of a very small cove. This cave was known to the Sechelt as SHAK'-KWOHT– a "bad" place. They say that long ago, when a storm gathered, lightning, SPUHK'-AHM, would strike here and a poison would be emitted. Travellers would give the spot a wide berth at such times. The Sechelt believed that if a person were to enter the cave at any time, he would die from the poisonous gas. Admittedly, the lightning action ceased many years ago but the name remains.

Long before white settlers came to the district, a medicine man chose SHAK'-KWOHT as a location for a rock painting. Perhaps he wished to show that his power was greater than that of the cave's poison. Upon visiting the spot, Basil Joe said he had been told many years before that the SEE-AY'-UHK could, indeed, withstand the destructive gases of the cave while others could not. In any case, the medicine man placed his insignia, a circle, at the cave entrance where it would be partially visible from the water. He painted something in the likeness of a salmon skeleton within the cave mouth and placed other symbols on the walls of the cave itself.

A geological survey of the area made some years ago showed a deposit of zinc sulfide at this spot. This particular legend could have a scientific basis; for the zinc compound, when more concentrated than it is now, might attract lightning. The resultant sulfurous fumes would be quite noxious.

Immediately round the point from this cave, and directly across the channel from Nelson Island's Green Bay, a steep shore consists of large, shingle-like rocks. Above this rough beach, a panel of light-gray granite, located at right angles to the waterway, displays three prominent symbols. One depicts a stylized deer, head uplifted and body almost erect, with forelegs held high. Just beyond this figure appears the likeness of a human skeleton. Beyond and above this second symbol is the twined Serpent, quite similar to that already referred to near the head of Salmon Arm.

When told of this mural, Reg Paull said that there was a story related to it. Once, Reg recounted, a Sechelt village beleaguered by raiders from the north was on the point of starvation. Suddenly, a deer appeared, walking erect and leading a small herd of its kind as a sacrificial gesture.

As with the stone statuette known as the Sechelt Image, the story may have been composed in comparatively recent times to fit a symbolic representation, the significance of which was not known to the general populace. There are no other Sechelt accounts of a village besieged by both water and land. Destructive raids, it would seem, took place only after the appearance of European liquor and muskets, and were invariably of short duration.

More significantly, the main symbol has a counterpart from distant antiquity. In ancient Sumer, archaeological diggings unearthed a golden figurine of a goat, walking erect and proffering a gift of food.[16] There, the symbolic figure seems analogous to the "scapegoat" that appeared to Abraham as he was about to sacrifice his son Isaac to his god.[17] Vignettes depicting deer, kneeling or erect, at a votive table in the form of a tau, have come down, carved or painted, from many parts of the ancient world. Here, the representation of the Serpent, TCHAIN'-KO, along with a stylized deer as in the Salmon Arm panel, seems to indicate a relationship between deer and human being which can be traced far back into mythology.

At the northern end of Agamemnon Channel, on a distinctive cliff at the entrance to Earl's Cove, two panels of paintings appear, one above the other. The most distinctive symbol here consists of concentric circles. Basil Joe said that this is the oldest pictograph known to the Sechelt. The circle, Basil said, represented a sign from their Divine Spirit, KWAHT-AHM-SAHTH'-AHM, that there would not be another Flood as that which had, ages ago, broken upon the people from Princess Louisa Inlet. To receive this sign, so Basil had been told, the SEE-AY'-UHK had travelled to NAH'-PATH, the "Place of Truth" in this inlet, where water trickled down over rock.

The circle represented a rainbow, said Basil, as seen in its entirety from a high place. In Germany, such a phenomenon is known as the Spectre of the Brocken, site of the Valpurgesnacht in the Harz Mountains, from which, under misty conditions, the rainbow appears as a complete circle. Basil knew that the symbolic rainbow in Agamemnon Channel, his people's LEAL'-KO-MAIN, antedated by a vast span of time any Biblical reference to Noah[18] learned by his people during the Christian era. "We had our own gods," said Basil.

About a mile and a half below the entrance to Vancouver Bay, SKWAH'-KWEE-AHM, two figures have been painted on the sheer rock above a ledge some forty feet above sea level. Each is about eighteen inches in height. The figures are humanoid, but with birdlike heads[19] in profile, much as Egyptian gods were depicted.[20] A solar halo appears above each figure, with rays emanating.

About three miles below Patrick Point, at the base of KWUH-OH'-TAH, where boys once leapt from the cliff as a manhood trial, a mass of symbols has been painted on the wall of a niche,[21] behind a natural rock formation. The rock formation is said to be shaped like the head of the White Whale, with open eye, emerging from the water. The painted symbols appear somewhat is the shape of small fishes. A rock floor would have provided sufficient space for whatever sort of ritual may have been held here.

There are other pictographs, with symbols not easily described, scattered around the Sechelt's traditional territory. They appear along the upper reaches of Jervis Inlet, near the B.C. Ferries terminal at Saltery Bay, at Alstrom Point, in the bay immediately north of the mouth of SAUGH'-AH-NAH, near the head of Hotham Sound, and in the upcoast corner of Quarry Bay, Nelson Island. Many secrets of these paintings were undoubtedly known only to the medicine man and were destined to die with his passing. It seems reasonable to presume, however, that all rock paintings embody something of aboriginal mythology. As in many cultures, the colour red possibly symbolized a power inherent in fearlessness or bravery – perhaps even in life itself.

Stories indicate the use of TUHM'-UHLTH, not only in war but also in hunting. In the tale of the hunter forced to his death from a narrow ledge high up the bluffs above SWEHN-AHL'-NAHM, his wife is said to have observed his falling body from her canoe below, "red against the gray rock." Since the skin of the Native Indian is not at all red by nature, and since neither fur not cedar-bark clothing would be red, it can be inferred that the mountain-goat hunter had painted his body that colour in preparation for his expedition, as hunters often did. In the scaling of sheer rock, where clothing would be cumbersome, the colour would be mixed with animal fat as a protection against extended exposure to cold.

A natural black earth colouring, WHEE'-OOKS, found high up in the mountains west of Narrows Arm, was also apparently used, particularly on the face above the cheekbones. On the smooth, hard shore of Nelson Island, just north of where Telescope Passage enters Jervis Inlet, a wide band of natural red exists at about eye-level for a man. The black coloration exists at about the remaining height of a man's head. The Sechelt have named this spot SKWUH-LAY'-KWUH-OHSS, which signifies the people, PAH'-LAY, of KWUH-OHSS', Vanguard Bay, with faces blackened.

Despite the little we know of these rock paintings, they represent almost the only contact we have today with the SEE-AY'-UHK, the most striking personage of the ancient Sechelt people.

To the extent that all aristocrats could create weapons and tools, and could add embellishment in form and colour, they were artists. Some, entitled to carve or paint through inheritance, and admitted to be more proficient than the others of their caste, were looked upon as specialists. The superiority was not, however, based on the proficiency itself. This proficiency came from a power, partially at least, inherent in the artist's Guardian Spirit. No subjective drive from within the individual gave him ability to create at will. The power came from a force from a realm of mysticism and spirituality, partially objectified by the mortal being.

The object of the artisan was not merely to create a functional bowl, or paddle, or canoe, or mask, although a well-carved artifact would serve its purpose. Nor was his object to create a thing of aesthetic beauty, although it might indeed become something of pleasing appearance.

The intention of the carver, or of the artist or the medicine man painter arose, not from any creative urge to fashion materials as he pleased, but from long-established custom, which prescribed the design both of the artifact and of its ornamentation. All true art results from and depends upon the involvement of the human being in a relationship to his or her surroundings. Each carved or pictured device represented some element of the fundamental beliefs of the people. Each creature symbolized some unique feature in the total body of myths and legends from which he could select.

Technology today is effectively destroying the very concept of figurative perception. Such expressions as "to run like a deer," "as strong as a bull," "the eye of an eagle," and others that compare a human trait to that of a respected creature of the wilds are being rendered increasingly meaningless by innovations in mechanical and electrical devices.

Basically, all true art results from and depends upon the involvement of the human being in some relationship to his or her surroundings. To the extent that such involvement is restricted or lost, so is art restricted and lost.

A people is always most completely involved with nature during the primitive phase of cultural development. Any tendency toward a creation of urbanization, with its resultant ruination of natural environments and its sophistication of behaviour patterns removes the individual from the direct contact with birds and beasts and gods which alone can produce true symbolic art.

Chapter Fourteen

There is evidence to suggest that most of the world's major religious cults made their influence felt throughout Jervis and Sechelt Inlets during an unremembered past.

One of the oldest of these is referred to by some writers as the Wisdom Philosophy.[1] This belief was based on the observation of an unvarying pattern of cycle and rhythm in living things on earth and in heavenly bodies far away. Aboriginal Sechelt certainly learned of and lived by relationships between solar and lunar time cycles and the effects of sun and moon on terrestrial life. While the sun regulated seasons of growth and ripening in the plant world, gestation coincided with predictable lunar time. The Sechelt also maintained an unwritten calendar that coordinated moon cycles and solar year.

The Solar-Lunar Cult would seem to have constituted a natural outgrowth of and addition to the Wisdom Philosophy. Aboriginal Sechelt did look upon sun and moon as sources of power. While they did not regard the two heavenly bodies as god and goddess, they did consider the sun, SEE-AY'-UHK, as masculine; and the moon, SHEHL'-SHEHL, as feminine.

The special mask of HAY-STAHL', the Bogey-Man magician, as carved by Reg Paull, depicts the full moon as a solid blue disc ringed by a white circle – the sun's corona at the solar eclipse. The moon is placed above the centre of the forehead, and flanked by silvery-yellow crescents.

Closely related to the moon cult among ancient peoples was a

mythology involving the Serpent or Dragon. Some peoples believed that a mating of the celestial Serpent or Dragon with the
moon created life. An association can therefore be seen between
the solar-lunar Cult and the Serpent cult. While there was no
suggestion among the Sechelt that TCHAIN'-KO, the Serpent,
took part in any cosmic process, its likeness did symbolize male
fertility. As god of the sea, TCHAIN'-KO, who could change form
and disappear at will, displayed characteristics reminiscent of
Poseidon[2] in classical Greek mythology.

The Sechelt recognized a total of three sea serpents. TCHAIN'-
KO, all-powerful, they made no mention of having ever seen.
They identified him only through events in which they believed
he had participated. A second monster, YAH-KYE-AH'-TCHIN,
had two dorsal vanes. Although apparently physical, it was too
powerful to be caught. A third sea creature, KO-KO-LAITCH'-
IHN, had three dorsal vanes with webbing between. According
to a story that came down to Reg Paull, the people of TSHOH'-
NYE once caught a KO-KO-LAITCH'-IHN in a cedar-rope fish-
net. Neither of these last two beings featured in myth or appeared
as symbols in aboriginal lore.[3]

Both Old and New Testaments refer to the Serpent as the
epitome of evil power. The Book of Revelation specifically equates
the Dragon with the Serpent.[4] Since Michael and his angels
fought the Serpent in Heaven, the Biblical reference denotes no
common earthly being.

Yet instances of sightings from many parts of the world continually reinforce old stories about the existence of physical
dragons. Sechelt references to the existence of both mythical and
actual monsters in their waters thus accord quite closely with
universal ancient beliefs. Sechelt accounts are unusual, however,
in that they attest to a concurrent existence of TCHAIN'-KO,
YAH-KYE-AY'-TCHAIN, and KO-KO-LAITCH'-IHN; the mythical with the real.

Whether designated as Dragon or as Serpent, this force came
to be portrayed in many parts of the world with the ears of a
horse.[5] Both the Chinese dragon and the Viking dragon ship
represent the mythical monster with horse ears, as do many
representations of the Sea Serpent.[6] The national emblem of
Wales is a dragon, but its ancient name designated the creature
as a "water horse."

The aboriginal Sechelt portrayed TCHAIN'-KO with ears like
those of a horse. They also had their own "water horse," TAH-
KAY-WAH'-LAH-KLASH. This was a beautiful white horse,

complete with black blanket and rein, which appeared in natural rock on the enormous cliff above and to the left of KOH-KWAH-LAIN'-AHM, Chatterbox Falls, at the head of Princess Louisa Inlet.[7] The Sechelt say that TAY-KAY-WAH'-LAH-KLASH emerged from the water,[8] just as the Welsh ceffyl dwr, the "water horse," emerged from Marchlyn Fawr, variously known as "Lake of the Great Horse."[9]

So too, MOOSE-MOOSE-SHAH'-LAH-KLASH, a cow that the Sechelt say emerged from her cave to walk about the village of KLYE'-EH-KWIHM at night, has her counterpart in Ireland, where "wild cattle" are reported to have been observed coming out of a lake called Llyn Eidwen.

A very ancient prototype is to be found in the cult "the Twin Spirits of the Serpents" that came to be known as the Cow Worship and was based on Isis.[10]

Once, so Basil Joe said, he had seen a feathered snake, a SUHSS-OOLTH'-KYE. It was a small snake, Basil said. It could leap through the air and it hissed loudly. Elderly persons, he said, had told him that this feathered snake was very poisonous. Such a creature inevitably invites association with Quetzalcoatl, Plumed Serpent-God of the ancient Aztecs. While the Sechelt granted SUHSS-OOLTH'-KYE no mythical significance, this adorned serpent was once well enough known in their aboriginal lore to be assigned a name.

The Greek Heracles – a name obviously derived from the goddess Hera, his patron – both contested the bull of Minos and slew the cattle of Geryon.[11] An image of Heracles, portrayed in a white robe, armed with the bow of Athena and facing the white bull, can hardly be ignored in a consideration of what the Sechelts called STUHM-TOH'-MISH, the archer, facing a charging white grizzly bear, MY'-OOK. For the charging beast presents a shape much nearer to that of a bull than of a bear. And the milk-white ageless quartz certainly suggests the bull of ancient Egyptian, Hebrew, Greek, and Persian mythologies[12] rather than the comparatively dark grizzly bear.

Such very ancient Greek terms as "potamus" and "tau" made their way to the Pacific Northwest, to be retained intact, both in sound and meaning, by aboriginal Sechelt. The twined-serpent Caduceus of Hermes appears among these people in like manner, not only in idea but also in visible pictograph form. Is it not possible, then, that the myth of Heracles and the white bull also found its way here, to be altered in time to bowman and bear?

To the peoples of Southeast Asia, the term "Ahm" or, variously

"Nahm," embraces Brahma, the Creator; Vishnu, the Preserver; and Siva, the Destroyer.[13] To the aboriginal Sechelt, NAHM encompassed a totality of these tripartite elements in the life cycle. TCHEN-AH'-WAHSS-IHN, "The Seat of the Gods," symbolized creation. KULSE, "Anchor Mountain," represented preservation of life from an overwhelming calamity. The "Eternity Rock" at KWAIT-OH'-SEE-AT, which will some day touch the nearby cliff to mark the end of humanity, signified destruction. Far back in time, the ancient Sechelt named their Divine Spirit KWAHT-AHM-SAHTH'-AHM. They also used the term AHM in AHM'-TUHN, the sea egg which could either sustain or destroy life, depending on how it was prepared, and in many other words. The French "le nom" and the English "omelette," borrowed from across the Channel, retain something of the significant aspects of these very old sounds.

Into uncounted ages past, the Serpent was associated by some ancient peoples with a tree. Danitic peoples, who fashioned their sea-going craft to resemble dragons, also pruned trees so that three central tops represented the soul, spirit, and body of the Divine Lotus. Four lower branches pointed to the cardinal points— north, south, east, and west—representative of the earth's four primary forces. Prehistoric Druids of Ireland and Scotland apparently fashioned certain of their sacred yew trees in this manner, as did tree cult adherents around the world. In the eighteenth century, Alexander Humboldt recorded the finding of a Draconic tree in the Canary Islands, said by him to be some two thousand years old. Spanish invaders found in America trees cut and trained to the sacred Hebdomad—three branches above four— so large that their hollowed trunks served as temples. Thomas Jefferson's home, Monticello, was designed to symbolize much ancient lore. A black walnut tree there that had been so pruned was visited by the Manaca Indians as a sacred place long after the tribe had been forced to migrate west from their native land.[14]

A section of a frieze from ancient Gordium in Phrygia, 6th century B.C., depicts two caprids feeding on the Tree of Life.[15] A carved ivory plaque from Assyria, 8th or 9th century B.C. portrays a king enthroned. His right hand grasps a flowered stem of a tree, another branch of which displays seven leaves, each with seven veins.[16]

The ancient Hebrews adopted the Tau cross into their alphabet. Shorn of its secondary branches, the primordial Tree of

Life, it assumed the form of two squares of the Mason, or Builder, back to back.

Fully branched, and with each of its seven candleholders flanged to represent the Divine Lotus, the tau became the Menorah, closely related to the ancient Narayana, the seven-headed serpent of ancient India.

Possibly thousands of miles from its nearest counterpart, the Jervis Inlet pictograph Menorah depicts a link between the lore, known as TAH'-OO, and the Serpent, TCHAIN'-KO.

Near the head of SKOO'-PAH, Salmon Arm, a pictograph adjacent to the Twined Serpent is composed of seven lines emerging downwards, alternately, from a central stem, much like a portion of a "herring-bone" pattern. This symbol is literally identical to that found on a beaker in Susa, and believed to have been painted somewhere between 5000 and 4000 B.C. If, as is believed by some archaeologists, this delineation from ancient Chaldea did symbolize the mythical Tree of Life, then its facsimile on the Pacific Coast of North America could certainly designate this same spiritual idea; for knowledge of the ingredients needed to form such a belief exist in Sechelt territory into this last quarter of the twentieth century.

Unquestionably, myths from portions of the world that saw continual turmoil suffered and became distorted. No logical reason was given to explain why the Greek Titan Prometheus was punished for having brought fire to mortal beings – even if, as some philosophers would have us believe, the purported fire symbolized sexual awareness.

In like manner, even by the time of the legendary Homer, a natural rock and tidal whirlpool off the coast of Italy had become, respectively, Scylla and Charybdis, female monsters who attempted to destroy Odysseus and his crew.[17]

So, too, during the Odyssey, an enraged Cyclops, a one-eyed giant, imprisoned the traveller and his men in a cave with the apparent intent to consume them at his leisure.[18]

Ancient peoples throughout such waters as the Mediterranean, whose shores saw much human violence, found supernatural evil around its perimeter as well. The aboriginal Sechelt, however, were seldom out of view of some benevolent guardian. Somewhere along every significant piece of water, and near some if not all pictographs, rock represented the essence of a departed god of Creation.

Perhaps, a thousand years before Homer, there was no serpent-haired Medusa, no Minotaur to which Greek youths and maidens must be sacrificed, and no Prometheus chained to the rock. In any case, two thousand years after the time of these horrors, the Sechelt still inhabited a benevolent world, in which even TCHAIN'-KO caused no real harm.

According to Sechelt lore, there was once an orchard of wild crab apple trees, KUH'-OH-PYE, planted in rows in a place known as YEE'-OOK, up the SKWAH'-KAH River. Since these people regularly travelled many miles up mountain valleys, and since the term YEE'-OOK designated great distance, it would seem that the orchard referred to was located somewhere beyond the ordinary designation of "far away."

In beliefs as old as the story of humanity, the apple symbolized death. In presenting Adam with an apple, Eve made his physical self mortal, subject to the scythe of time.[19] All neolithic paradises were apparently orchard-islands. In its oldest sense, the word "paradise" meant "orchard."

Readers of the *Iliad* may recall the episode in which Paris, son of King Priam of Troy, presented an apple to Aphrodite, Goddess of Love, the apple on which the Goddess of Discord had inscribed the phrase "For the fairest." But it would seem that far back before Homer's age, it was Aphrodite who presented the apple to Paris. This symbolized his admission after death to the Elysian Fields, the apple orchards of the West, to which only the souls of heroes were admitted.

Closest to the aboriginal Sechelt's lore is the classic Greek account of the Hesperides. Those were nymphs who, with the aid of a dragon, guarded an orchard in which golden apples grew. Theft of these apples figured in popular mythology as one of the labours of Hercules.[20] However, Robert Graves, who immersed himself over many years in primitive and ancient myths and legends concluded that the three goddesses presented the hero with an apple of immortality–of perpetual life after death.[21]

According the Sechelt legend, several miles up the SKWAH'-KAH, there existed the SUHSS-OOLTH'-KYE, the poisonous plumed serpent. Far up this same canyon–which was impassable, as was the way to the golden grove of the Hesperides–stood the apple orchard of YEE'-OOK. Whether or not any long-lost story interwove the three phenomena, the fact remains that references to the Tree, the Serpent, and the Apple–all universal symbols–are to be found in and beyond the upper reaches of Jervis Inlet.

Kindred of the aboriginal Sechelt's Thunderbird, Raven, and Condor can be traced far back into the myths of other peoples. In ancient Egypt, perhaps long before the advent of Osiris, the Phoenix symbolized a cycle of death and resurrection. According to Arabic mythology, the Roc was a giant bird that frequented the Indian Ocean. From southern Asia, the Gryphon–part lion, part eagle, with a serpent's tail–made its way into European mythology, along with the one-eyed people of Scythia. In ancient Scandinavian lore, the Svalbard was the Serpent Bird of the mythical rhythm of Valhalla. Undoubtedly, the Norse bard sand not only of historic events but also of magical things beyond the world of man. The eagle made its way into ethnic heraldry to such an extent that its likeness appears–usually with wings outspread–on many contemporary national flags and seals.

While the Sechelt paid no special homage to the eagle, they did adopt certain birds–the raven and the condor–into their mythology. Mythological Raven was seen as an incredibly huge and powerful creature, completely separated in concept from the actual bird.[22] They sculptured the Condor atop totem poles, in true likeness, as a symbol of the human psyche.

The term KWAHT-KAY'-AHM can be variously translated to mean either Thunderbird or Thundergod,[23] the supernatural being whose earth-shaking voice came from the sky. The Thunderbird was depicted with a human face and bird's tail, but with parts of the anatomy arranged in stylized form that no composite of the mythical creature could be logically synthesized in the mind. Such a stylization comports with universal belief that the form of god must not be seen.

Literally all of the earth's mythologies refer to origins "from the sky." Folklore, stone carvings, and manuscripts reveal remarkable similarities in accounts of creation and human origin from almost all peoples of the globe. In one way or another, a Creator God or Divine Spirit from the heavens above brought original members of a people–usually divine but mortal creatures–into being.

In societies such as those of ancient Egypt and Mycenae, only royal and aristocratic figures were prepared for an afterlife. More often, in succeeding cultures, all souls fortunate enough to have received approved ceremonious dispatch could be expected to go to some sort of safe haven. In varying degrees among different beliefs, souls of malefactors or of those whose fate remained uncertain could not hope to fare so well.

In those cultures where the criminal is permitted to remain in or to return to society, concern for disposition of the soul has been de-emphasized through many centuries past.

Since evildoers were expelled from social groups among peoples of the Pacific Northwest, all remaining persons could expect their souls barring theft by some evil agent, to reach a place of eternal peace.

Early Christian missionaries to this coast reported that they had found a vague pantheism[24] in Native beliefs. Yet the cycle of life was probably visualized more clearly by the aboriginal Sechelt than it was by the peoples of Europe who sent their clergymen here. A new life was not born in sin. Individuals, when young, would be told of their divine origin. At death, they could expect both immortality for their souls and perpetuation of their very selves through perpetuation of their names.

Had early missionaries been able to penetrate aboriginal myth, they would have found many beliefs fundamentally quite similar to their own,[25] even though ceremonies differed. Had members of the clergy arrived at the Pacific Northwest, without an accompanying European population and technology, it is quite possible that the superficial differences inherent in the Old World idea of God and the Sechelt's idea of their Divine Spirit, KWAHT-AHM-SAHTH'-AHM, would have been reconciled without much change in the tempo of their daily lives.

Decimation of their people by the ravages of smallpox during the last half of the nineteenth century forced councils of the chief villages to turn to Christianity. By 1860, it became clear that neither Native remedies nor the powers of the shaman, the SEE-AY'-UHK, could prevent the obliteration of the people from extraneous diseases brought to these shores. In desperation, chiefs and their councils turned for help to other Europeans—to the medicines of doctor and nurse and to the spiritual guidance of the Christian priest.[26] When they accepted Christianity, the Sechelt leaders were constrained to abolish their shamans and to discontinue their traditional sacred occasions.

As the era of the SEE-AY'-UHK and the KLUHN-UHN'-AHK ended, so did that of the HAY'-WOHSS, the hereditary chief. As the population was reduced from several thousand to only a few hundred, the old ways of life based on initiation, festival, and ceremony, with almost every daily act part of a mystic ritual, simply could not endure throughout the great reaches of Sechelt and Jervis inlets.

Even before the crisis of depopulation precipitated the end of aboriginal structures, other forces were subtly working to destroy life as it had prevailed for uncounted years.

As far back as 1786, James Stuart Strange commented in his

journal that the Native Indians at the northern tip of Vancouver Island possessed no iron that he could see, but that they did express a desire for iron implements and utensils.[27] He had named this headland Cape Scott before Europeans knew for certain that the land mass south of it was indeed an island. Steel axes, chisels, and knives could cut and carve more quickly than traditional stone tools could. Iron pots, which could be placed directly in a fire, were obviously superior to wooden bowls or boxes, into which heated stones must be dropped to boil water for cooking.

In 1792, Captain George Vancouver noticed muskets of Spanish manufacture in the lodge of Chief Cheslakee, near the mouth of the Nimpkish River in the northern part of Vancouver Island. Firearms, which could be obtained in exchange for furs, quickly replaced the bow and arrow and the lance as weapons throughout the coast, long before those who acquired them turned to Christianity.

In 1800, Chief Macquilla—called Maquinna by Europeans—perceiving the destructive effects the fur trade was having on his hereditary institutions, slaughtered the crew of the Yankee trading vessel *Boston* in a futile attempt to halt the change.[28]

The Sechelt were not broken in upon by miners, as Interior peoples were, and did not move to any established fort. From stories told, however, it would appear they were using at least some of the white man's weapons, tools and utensils before the middle of the nineteenth century.

When, then, chiefs felt compelled to relinquish their ancestral religion, they must have realized the fact that, while the ravages of smallpox may have determined the time of the turn to Christianity, other forces were are work that would in any case slowly but surely erode the aboriginal culture.

When the conversion to Christianity occurred, the Sechelt war-chief could not break from his old way of life. According to Reg Paull, the war chief, SKY'-AKTH, was always TSOHT-TSOHT-LOH'-MATTSOHT; that is, he was looking for more spirit power, which he believed he could attain from other people who died by his hand. This man was so ferocious that during times of peace, he was not permitted to mingle with his people. At various places apart from regular village sites, special lodges were provided for this unruly but essential person. Lonely and always on the move, he traditionally wandered from one of these places to another, taking no part in his people's daily affairs, but always ready to lead in times of war.

When the Sechelt took to Christianity, TSUH-KAHL', who had led warriors in the rescue of WHEE'-PUHL-AH-WIT, was still war chief. Unable to accept a life of peace, TSUH-KAHL' teamed with TCHEW-HAY'-LAHM, of Chemainus, one of his co-leaders in the retributary raid of years before. From a Gulf Island hideaway, trying desperately to perpetuate their aboriginal roles, these two great mean undertook a last-ditch stand against all the forces of cultural change. For a time, they waylaid and killed travellers, Native Indian as well as European, who happened to pass their way.

The death of TSUH-KAHL'—through violence, as he had lived— marked the end of the aboriginal Sechelt Nation more dramatically than any other event could have done.

A century later, descendants of that shattered people, looking constantly to both past and future, have brought into being a new nation.

Notes

CHAPTER ONE

1. Tom MacInnes, *Chinook Days.* Vancouver: Sun Publishing Co. Ltd., 1935, p. 65.

2. Immanuel Velikovsky, *Earth In Upheaval.* New York: Dell Publishing Co. Inc., 1955, p. 113. Referring to the Ice Age, the author says, "Falling again and again in a sunless world, the snow, shielded from the sun's rays by thick clouds enveloping the earth, would finally cool the ground to the point where it would turn, not into water, but into ice."

3. Information obtained from Grant Keddie, Extension Archaeologist, Provincial Museum, Victoria, British Columbia.

4. Genesis 6 et. seq.

5. James Churchward, *The Sacred Symbols of Mu.* New York: Ives Washburn, 1944, p. 140. An illustration is entitled "The Divine Hennes Boat: The flight of the soul to the region of incarnation. The deceased is sailing his bark through the field of stars to Amenti, the domain of Osiris, for judgment and reincarnation."

6. Eloise Hart, "The Prophet of Light," *Sunrise,* ed. Grace Knoche. Pasadena: The Theosophical Press, February 1977, p. 175: "*Ameretat,* associated with the mystic Tree of Life, the immortality which frees one from the fear of death."

7. Blair A. Moffett, "One Foot in the Fifth World," *Sunrise,* January 1975, p. 120: "These Ayar-Incas traced their origin to an emergence from 'the Cave of Pararitambo' following a flood."

8. See *Lillooet Stories,* Sound Heritage, Vol. VI, Number 1. Victoria, Provincial Archives, R.W.J. Langlois, ed., 1977. The first story in the collection is entitled "The Flood."

9. Exodus 10:22 and Joshua 10:12,13.
10. Immanuel Velikovsky, op.cit. The theme of cataclysm induced by the intrusion of a cosmic body runs throughout the book.
11. Charles Hill-Tout, *The Great Fraser Midden*. Vancouver Art, Historical and Scientific Association, 1908.
12. Roy Carlson, "The Archaeological Explosion in B.C." *Westworld*, April–May, 1977, p. 17.
13. Donated by William Peterson to Elphinstone Pioneer Museum, Gibsons, British Columbia.
14. Carbon-14 dating of charcoal from a pit barbecue on Santa Rosa Island, off the coast of California near Santa Barbara, confirmed the presence of man at that site at least 40,000 years ago: Rainer Berger, *Science News* (March 26, 1977), p. 96. J.L. Bada, R.A. Schroeder, and G.F. Carter report that dates deduced from the extent of amino acid racemization in human remains from six California sites suggest that man was present at least 50,000 years before the present: *Science*, Vol. 184, p. 791–3, (May 17, 1974). Archaeological methods have indicated probable ages of over 100,000 years for artifacts found in California and Arizona. These discoveries are pertinent to considerations of the age of man anywhere in North America.
15. Charles Hill-Tout, Journal of the Anthropological Institute, Vol. 34, 1904, p. 311. The professor, referring to Native Indians living along the Harrison River, a tributary of the Fraser, said that they were a "somewhat modified remnant of the race that occupied these regions prior to the advent of the Salish, who we know are an intrusive people and comparative latecomers."
16. Pierre Grimal, ed., *World Mythology*, translated by Patricia Beardsworth. London: The Hamlyn Publishing Group Ltd., 1974, p. 97.
17. See *The Nag Hammadi Library in English*, ed. James M. Robinson, New York: Harper and Row, 1977. The Gnostics believed that the Divine Mind created the Aeon, architects of the Cosmos, and the Archons, the builders immersed in substance and producing material vehicles for the ongoing creation. Like Vishnu, the Divine Spirit was "the dreamer of the world illusion."
18. John Mitchell, *The View Over Atlantis*, New York: Ballantine Books, 1969, p. 53: "A great many hills, rocks and mounds, of which Wrekin and Silbury are but two examples out of hundreds, are supposed according to local legends to have been set down on the landscape by a former race of earth-moving giants."
19. Even the traditional account of Creation in the Old Testament makes no specific reference to God's having brought the waters into being. Genesis 1:10 specifies earth to mean dry land.
20. Thor Heyerdahl, *American Indians of the Pacific*, London: George Allen & Unwin Ltd., 1952, p. 237. Cf. Leviticus 16:2.
21. J.S. Matthews, *Conversations With Khahtsahlano, 1932–1954*. Vancouver City Archives, 1955, p. 90.
22. H.P. Blavatsky, *The Secret Doctrine*. Pasadena: The Theosophic-

al Society Press, 1974, Vol. I, p. 141 and passim. Madam Blavatsky states that the Titans were giants of the Third Root Race, associated with the god Atlas. At varying times, the author notes, Hercules was accorded such diverse roles as Apollonian Sun-God and Promethean Titan.

23. See Ellen Raynard, *Stones Crying Out*. London: The Book Society, 1880, p. 239. The author refers to an ancient Israelite cemetery at Kibroth-Hattaavah (Numbers 11:33,34), where the figures of goats abound on tombstones raised over the graves of people who had died after eating birds she believed were red-legged cranes, soon after the Exodus from Egypt.

24. Cyrus H. Gordon, *Before Columbus*. Philadelphia: Chilton Book Co., 1966, p. 150.

25. Ibid., p. 137.

26. Exodus 17:6.

27. Sir James George Frazer, *The Golden Bough*, Abridged Edition. London: MacMillan & Co. Ltd., 1967, p. 5.

28. Thor Heyerdahl, op.cit., pp. 154, 741.

29. Franz Boas, "The Social Organization of the Kwakiutls." *Report of National Museum of Canada*, 1895.

30. The Sechelt never gave these protoancestors any fixed form. As in the lore of ancient Greece and elsewhere, they were attributed human embodiment in one story and supernatural characteristics in another.

31. One bit of lore tells of a bear having been seen, as recently as well into the twentieth century, entering the sea and transforming into a ferocious monster, YAH-KAH-AY'-TCHEEN.

32. Warren Smith, *Lost Cities of the Ancients Unearthed*. New York: Kensington Publishing, 1976, p. 53: "The Spanish National Archives contain an old manuscript that tells of a sea serpent being swept up on the beaches of Santa Maria del Mar, Oaxaca, Mexico, in 1648 . . . 'It was a dreadful monster that was tossed up on the beach by the waves,' reads the manuscript. 'The people of the village saw it at daybreak after a storm. . . . These people were terrified because they saw it move and flop about on the sand. But as the day passed, the motion became less. . . . It was 15 *yaras* (41 feet) in length and 6 feet in height lying on the sand. The body was covered with a reddish-brown pelt like that of a cow. It had two forefeet...'"

33. Henri Frankfort, et al., *Before Philosophy*, Penguin Books, 1949, p. 22. The ancient Egyptians, the author says, believed that their arts and crafts had come from their god Osiris.

CHAPTER TWO

1. This ambivalence shown by the aboriginal Sechelt toward the whale and other creatures from the real and mythological world may

be expressed by the word "awe," a term that signifies mixed reverence and fear.

2. During the early nineteenth century, California condors were still seen as far north as the Columbia River. See Carl B. Koford, *The California Condor*, New York: Dover Press, 1952, p. 8.

3. Alan W. Watts, *The Two Hands of God*, New York: Collier Books, 1964, p. 13. "The gods are the archetype, but they exist as perpetually incarnate in ourselves," says Watts.

4. The figures on the pole carved by Reg Paull might be said to symbolize what in Buddhism is known as a "Wisdom of the Yonder Shore." In that belief, the representation is not psychological phenomena common to all individuals but of the acquisition of wisdom by those candidates selected for admission into the sacred mysteries. At the culmination of the aboriginal Sechelt's Guardian Spirit Quest, as Reg explained it, the initiate attained a vision of ultimate realization; the unity of matter, as symbolized by the Serpent, and spirit, as indicated by the Condor with wings outstretched.

5. Leviticus 5:15; 24:14 et seq.

6. A. S. Bhaktivedanta Swami Prabaryada, *Bhagavad-Gita As It Is*, Abridged Edition. Los Angeles: Bhaktivedanta Book Trust, p. 266, #51–53.

7. Hereditary Chief Reg Paull gave this appositive definition. See William Shakespeare's *Macbeth*, act 1, sc. 4, in which the protagonist says,

> Stars, hide your fires!
> Let not light see my black and deep desires:
> The eye wink at the hand! Yet let that be
> Which the eye fears, when it is done, to see.

8. Matthew 5:40, 41.

9. Victor Hugo, *Les Miserables*.

10. Alexander Dumas, *The Count of Monte Cristo*.

11. Job 41.

12. Alan W. Watts, op. cit., p. 45: "To say that opposites are polar is to say that they are related and joined – that they are the terms, ends, or extremities of a single whole."

13. Numbers 21:9.

14. Joseph Campbell, *The Masks Of God: Creative Mythology*, New York: The Viking Press, 1970, p. 154. "Whenever nature is revered as self-moving, and so inherently divine, the serpent is revered as symbolic of its divine life," says the author.

15. Cyrus H. Gordon, op. cit., p. 198. The author notes that the ancient Etruscans did not distinguish "k" from "g" phonetically. The Sechelt did not use a true "g" sound. In their name for Jervis Inlet, LEG-OH'-MAIN, the "g" hovers between a "g" and a "k" sound. The

Sechelt also did not use sounds. that would require the "b," the "d," the "f," the "q," the "r," the "v," the "x," or the "z" of our alphabet.

16. Barry Fell, *America, B.C.* New York: Demeter Press, 1976, p. 147. This page displays a photo of a rock found in central Vermont in 1975 and thought to be an ancient Celtic herm. Fell believes that this figure may have represented the Celtic goddess Byanu, personification of all womankind. Although the natural stone figure known to the Sechelt as a portrayal of Mink is much larger than the Vermont herm, it resembles the shape of the smaller image very closely. Perhaps Mink was once a Creator rather than a Transformer in Sechelt mythology.

17. Pierre Grimal, et al., op. cit., p. 98.

18. Revelations 10:5,6: "And the angel which I saw stand upon the sea sware . . . that there should be time no longer."

19. Henri Frankfort, et al., op. cit., p. 60. The pyramid, synonymous with the hill, signifies order from chaos, say the authors.

20. H.P. Blavatsky, op. cit., Vol. II, p. 362. According to a writer of ancient times, says the author, a pyramid was the tomb of Seth, proto-god of Egypt.

CHAPTER THREE

1. British Columbia Heritage Series, *Introduction to Our Native People*, Victoria Provincial Archives, 1966, p. 16.

2. Homer G. Barnett, *The Coastal Salish of British Columbia.* University of Oregon Press, 1955, p. 2.

3. Charles Hill-Tout, *The Native Races of the British Empire: British North America: The Far West, the Home of the Salish and Dene,* Archibald Constable & Co. Ltd., 1907, p. 25 and passim.

4. *Dictionary of Chinook Jargon.* Victoria: T.N. Hibben & Co., 1899, Reprinted 1972.

5. R.C. Mayne, *Four Years in British Columbia and Vancouver Island.* London: John Murray, 1862, p. 244.

6. A.G. Morice, OMI, *History of the Catholic Church in Western Canada (1659–1895).* Toronto: The Musson Book Co. Ltd., 1910, p. 377.

CHAPTER FOUR

1. Edmund, S. Meany, *Vancouver's Discovery of Puget Sound,* Portland: Binfords & Mort, 1957, pp. 85, 123.

2. Ibid.

3. Information passed down to the late Chief Reg Paull.

4. Some of these finds are now in Elphinstone Pioneer Museum, Gibsons.

5. Homer G. Barnett, op. cit., p. 9.

6. Denys Nelson, *Fort Langley 1827–1927.* Vancouver: Arts Historical and Scientific Association, 1927, p. 7.

7. *A Journal Kept At Nootka During the Years 1803–1805.* Boston: C.E. Goodspeed, 1931.

8. Adriane Ruskin and Michael Batterberry, *Greek and Roman Art.* New York: McGraw-Hill, 1968, pp. 79, 80.

9. 1 Kings 6, 7.

10. H.P. Blavatsky, op. cit., Vol. I, p. 5. The Tau –T– says the author, is the symbol of the androgynous Third Root Race.

11. Tom MacInnes, op. cit., pp. 34, 35. Native Indians told MacInnes that Tah-oo meant "spiritual distance."

12. *Hamlet*, act 2, sc. 2, line 584.

13. See H.P. Blavatsky, op. cit., Vol. II, p. 139.

14. Ibid., p. 520.

15. See Bullfinch's *Mythology.*

16. Matthew 7:12

CHAPTER FIVE

1. Pierre Grimal, et al. *op. cit.*, p. 369.

2. Exodus 24:29

CHAPTER SIX

1. Thomas Crosby, *Up and Down the North Pacific Coast by Canoe and Mission Ship.* Frederick Clarke Stephenson, 1914.

2. R.C. Mayne, op. cit., p. 61.

3. See Fosco Maraini, *Meeting With Japan.* New York: Viking Press, 1959, p. 98: "A Japanese is not an individual; he is a cog in a delicate social mechanism."

4. R.C. Mayne, op. cit., p. 61.

5. H.P. Blavatsky, op. cit. Vol. I., p. 17 and passim.

6. See Leviticus 23.

7. See Leonhard Adam, *Primitive Art.* Penguin Books, 1949, p. 63.

8. John Mitchell, *op. cit.*, p. 128: "The 12th century scholar Ramon Lull, ascending Mount Randa in Majorca to spend some days in fasting and meditation, gazed at a lenticus bush, covered with little silvery leaves. As he watched, on each leaf appeared a letter or number, until the bush displayed every letter and sign in every language known to men. The various sciences united in one sublime system."

9. Robert Graves, *The White Goddess.* London: Faber and Faber Ltd., 1962, p. 359. The writer suggests here that the wolf that nurtured Romulus and Remus in mythological Roman times was actually human. The myth of the "werewolf," according to which the "wer" (man) was, under certain lunar conditions, transformed into a wolf, must be looked upon as a parallel to this aboriginal Sechelt legendary phenomenon.

10. See Benjamin Lee Whorf, *Language, Thought, and Reality.* Cambridge: the M.I.T. Press, 1956, p. 63. Referring to the Hopi Indian

concept of time and space, Whorf says, "If it does not happen 'at this place', it does not happen 'at this time'; it happens at 'that' place at 'that' time.

11. Joseph Campbell, op. cit., p. 118. The author notes that in ancient China the tiger was considered a guardian, not an antagonist.

12. Robert Graves, op. cit., p. 414. The mystery of Ezekiel's vision was taught to only the wise novitiate, says Graves, with no one but master and candidate present.

13. John Collier, *Indians of the Americas*. Mentor, 1947, p. 21: "Native Indians assumed that intensity of consciousness—concentrated, sustained longing and the feeling of power, joy, happiness, beauty, and the union with the forces of being—was effectual in the magical control of nature through co-partnership with the gods."

14. Artifact tools and weapon points, some very old, have been found in geologically stable areas of the world. Even though these pieces would accumulate indefinitely, since stone endures throughout ages, they appear in such extensive quantities that their users could hardly have all lived in caves, the nearest of which are often miles away.

15. Plato, *The Timaeus*, Thomas Taylor translation. The Bollingen Series, Pantheon Books, 1944, pp. 98–99. At a certain periodic ceremony, according to the philosopher, children's names were added to the list in ancient Athens.

16. Leonhard Adam, op. cit., p. 64. Adam says that the Guardian Spirit Dance portrayed the initiate's "death," with rebirth to spiritual power.

17. These submissions to water closely paralleled in purpose the age-old ritual of baptism, from which a person emerged as a "new" spiritual being. The aboriginal Sechelt trials advanced the initiate toward both physical and spiritual maturity.

18. The candles that adorn the heads of girls in Sweden at a Christmas ceremony and those carried by participants in the February 2nd Christian Candlemas also give light, but the shedding of physical light is not their prime purpose in these rituals. Nor was the fire in the Sechelt's ceremonial PUHN'-AHW-TWUH kindled merely for warmth and physical illumination.

19. See Pierre Gimal, et al., op. cit., pp. 192, 193. The essential part of the Mazdean Cult of ancient Persia, the sacrificial liturgy *Yasna*, took place in the presence of fire, Grimal notes.

CHAPTER SEVEN

1. Pierre Grimal, et al., op. cit., p. 241 and plate opposite. The Hindu god Siva is depicted here in a stylized dance step symbolic of regeneration into a higher spiritual plane.

2. The similarity of this word to KWAHT-AHM-SAHTH'-AHM, the Sechelt's Divine Spirit, would seem to indicate that the haven to which souls would normally go was associated with this Supreme Being.

3. See Sir James George Frazer, op. cit., p. 244.
4. Ibid., p. 247.
5. Ibid., p. 878 et seq.
6. Leonhard Adam, op. cit., p. 156.
7. Genesis 2:7.
8. Genesis 19:26.
9. See Bullfinch, op. cit.
10. Leonhard Adam, op. cit. p. 55. The writer uses the popular term "mana" to mean a "soul-substance."
11. Tom MacInnes, op. cit., p. 35. MacInnes believed that this word may have originated at Nootka Sound during its occupation by Spain. Since, however, the author himself discovered that Nootka Indians knew of the *Tao-te-ching*, then it is possible that the same contact who had brought them that teaching also brought them the term "mana," if indeed it was not already here from some unknown age before.
12. As "aye" denotes affirmation, and "my," as in "mycosia," denotes a destructive element.
13. See Sir James George Frazer, op. cit., p. 874.
14. Exodus 7:19 et seq.
15. Joseph Campbell, op. cit., pp. 116, 117. The Queller of Beasts, as characterized and portrayed here, appeared in physical likeness, says Campbell, at least as far back as 1600 B.C., in the form of a man, on a Cretan seal, calming two lions, not physically, but with psychic power.

CHAPTER EIGHT

1. John Sharkey, *Celtic Mysteries*. London, Thames and Hudson, 1975, p. 5. Ancient Celtic peoples maintained oral traditions, the author says, and placed taboos against writing by all but the Druid class.
2. See H.P. Blavatsky, op. cit., Vol. II, p. 565.
3. Leonhard Adam, op. cit., p. 130. The author mentions similar discontinuations of anatomy in ornamentation on marble vessels excavated on the banks of the River Ulua in Honduras, and ascribed to the second great period of Mayan civilization—eleventh to twelfth century A.D.
4. Huntington Cairns, *Law and the Social Sciences*. New York: Harcourt, Brace & Co., 1935, p. 21. Property, in primitive societies, says the author, is "basically conceived of as a part of the personality or self; it is a relation between the maker and his work."
5. See R.C. Mayne, op. cit., p. 73 and passim.

CHAPTER NINE

1. See F.W. Howay, and E.O.S. Scholefield, *British Columbia*. Vancouver: S.J. Clarke Publishing Co., 1914, Vol. I, p. 175. The Coast Salish cod lure is described as a wooden cone with strips of bark attached to

140 Notes to Chapter Ten

its periphery, like the feathers of a shuttlecock. The authors say that some Native peoples used sharpened mussel-shell tips to their spears.

2. In a letter written February 12, 1980, John Sibert, Research Scientist, Pacific Biological Station, Nanaimo, commented on this point "Large sea creatures may indeed live indefinitely if there is food and if they do not meet a violent end. The question becomes how long is indefinite? Surely a million years is unreasonable. Large scale catastrophic events (earthquake, sudden alterations in ocean circulation) occur at that time scale and would make life difficult for such a creature. On the other hand, large trees may live 1000 years. Perhaps 1000 to 2000 years could be a reasonable *guess* at the long part of longevity."

3. Alwyn and Brinley Rees, *Celtic Heritage*. London: Thames and Hudson, 1961, p. 246.

4. See Leviticus 11.

5. The Sechelt SHEHL-AYL'-TUHN has, far away, a counterpart in the traditional Irish cedgel, the shillelagh, once also, perhaps, thrown as a weapon.

6. Information received from George Glassford, son-in-law to George Gibson, founder of Gibson's Landing.

7. Robert Graves, op. cit., p. 293. The Ark of the Covenant was covered with porpoise skin, says Graves, and the porpoise was one of the three royal "fish" of Britain.

8. The Paull family retained—and perhaps still retain—a carved soapstone headpiece, their ancestral "coronet," which was once held in place on the forehead of a TAH-WAHN'-KWUH chief by means of a leather strap. It was made with deep, narrow holes drilled along the rim, for the insertion of sea-lion bristles, so Reg said.

9. Such an account, timeless, and handed down orally from generation to generation, reveals one way in which a creature from nature may become a family heraldic figure. It also suggests that, all around the world, "stories" that appear to have taken place within the identifiable history of a people are often actually myths, roving back in time to cultural beginnings.

CHAPTER TEN

1. Charles P. Smith, noted Pacific Northwest collector, concluded early in his career, during the 1920s, that stone hammers were once mythologically significant, and that many had been ruined deliberately.

2. A period of unrest among Interior Indians followed signing of the Oregon Treaty in 1846. The 49th Parallel, established as the boundary between U.S. and British interests in the Northwest, cut through traditional Native territories. When conflicts affected the Lillooet, some of them sought refuge among their coastal neighbours, perhaps taking along some jade articles. The greatest accumulation of jade artifacts, however, was discovered along a very short length of shore-

line, east of Egmont Point, at the confluence of Sechelt and Jervis inlets. Such a concentration of like objects at this site suggests the possibility that they originated as trade items from some place oceans away.

3. The reliance on the physical and imaginative visions probably best distinguishes art from science throughout the world. Any object, even one destined for functional use, made without measurement of any kind can be classified as a work of art.

4. In Hubert Evans' classic *Mist on the River*, the young protagonist, after a prolonged inner conflict regarding his identity, decides, while he is helping a hereditary carver to spread and launch a canoe, to remain with his people on the shores of the Skeena River.

5. Reg Paull said that he could not divulge the meaning of this cleft in the canoe's prow. Undoubtedly, the term "fox-nose" is a descriptive name given by Europeans familiar with the fox, an animal foreign to Sechelt legend. From the appearance of some canoes, it would seem likely that the prow presented the head and neck of the Serpent, TCHAIN'-KO, god of the sea, while the canoe represented the body. This kind of symbolism is also found in the Viking "Dragon" ships.

6. Robert Graves, op. cit., p. 22. "In ancient Ireland, the *ollave*, or master-poet, sat next to the king at table and was privileged, as none else but the queen was, to wear six different colours in his clothes," says the writer.

7. P.P. Kahane, *Ancient and Classical Art*, translated by Robert Erich Wolf. New York: Dally Publishing Co., Inc., 1968, p. 11. Prehistoric paintings, says the author, are "high art"—made by a fixed upper social class.

8. The Greek god-goddess Hermes Aphrodite portrayed sexual duality. Aphrodite was customarily associated with her child, Eros, the boy on the dolphin.

CHAPTER ELEVEN

1. The foregoing ethnobotanical names appear as given in 1962 by the late Basil Joe of Sechelt. In 1972, eight years after the death of Basil, Nancy Turner of the University of British Columbia prepared a list of Sechelt plant names obtained from other informants.

2. Robert Graves, op. cit. p. 426. Graves says that both *A Midsummer Night's Dream* and *The Tempest*, though presented on stage as comedies, are filled with ancient lore and mythological figures once common to peoples from Egypt to Britain.

3. Act 2, sc. 1, lines 165–172.

CHAPTER TWELVE

1. Benjamin Lee Whorf, op. cit., p. 57 et seq.

2. Two drowning incidents involving Native British Columbia Indians occurred within a few days of each other during the summer of

1959. A child fell into the Thompson River near Kamloops, and two youths were swept away when their car plunged into the Nicola near Merritt. After conventional methods had failed to locate the bodies, the Indians resorted to the powers of a very elderly Native seer. He "saw" the bodies, in both instances in locations contrary to where currents would in all probability have carried them. The bodies were recovered for burial.

3. Tom MacInnes, op. cit., p. 35.

4. Robert Rensselaer, "Renovation Follows Renovation Without Cease," *Sunrise*, ed. Grace Knoche. Pasadena, November, 1976, p. 57. The author quotes from the *Tao-te-ching* of Lao-tzu. The first line of the poem reads, "The Tao that can be expressed is not the eternal Tao."

5. A sort of metonymy, the term SKOH'-MYE serves for both "year" and "snow," there being essentially one "snow" in each year.

6. Cyrus H. Gordon, op. cit. p. 136. The author notes that the Mayan and Egyptian calendars consist of 360 days plus 5 intercalary days that are not included in the monthly structure of the year.

7. H.P. Blavatsky, op. cit., Vol. I, p. 362. The author refers to an account by Herodotus, who said that there were two kinds of ibis, one all black and one black and white. The Egyptians held the black and white ibis sacred to Isis, the moon goddess. There are two varieties of gold-eye duck in the Pacific Northwest. One is a mottled brown, and the other, the Barrows Gold-Eye, is mixed black and white.

8. It would see that the Sechelt continued to count the days in intervals of seven, ignoring the increasing discrepancy with lunar cycles until the end of the year.

9. The sun was KWUH-OH-TAH; "straight up," at noon, as was the cliff thus named from which boys dove into Jervis Inlet as one of their manhood initiation trials.

10. Approximately 200 billion gallons during each tidal change.

CHAPTER THIRTEEN

1. Vernon, Wayside Press Ltd.

2. P.P. Kahane, op. cit., p. 8. The author mentions pictographs in the Franco-Cantabrian mountain area dating back to about 13,500 B.C.

2a. See *The Norton Anthology of English Literature*, Third Edition. W.W. Norton & Company Inc., New York, 1975, p. 2371. An editorial footnote here says, "The dolphin, in ancient art, was a symbol of the soul in transit from one state to another."

3. John Mitchell, op. cit., p. 35. "According to this legend, the holy places, the sites of ancient and traditional sanctity, were first revealed in the performance of a magical rite, through some divine omen, in dreams or visions."

4. Alwyn and Brinley Rees, op. cit., p. 79. Participants at a ritual in ancient India saw the highest stride of Vishnu as a fixed eye in heaven. They kindled a fire – symbolically, Vishnu at an altar.

5. John Sharkey, op. cit. p. 18. In an ancient Celtic ceremony, says the author, white marked stones were placed in a fire. When they had cooled, each candidate drew from the ashes the stone marked with his identifying symbol.

6. Joseph Campbell, op. cit. p. 97. A plate shows the likeness of an Orphic bowl from the second or third century A.D. A winged serpent is seen atop the Orphic egg, within which all mortal creatures dwell.

7. H. Aynsley-Murray, *Symbolism of the East and West*. London: George Pedway, 1900. Mrs. Aynsley-Murray believed that painted pebbles found in caves from India to the shores of northern Europe were representations of the sacred egg.

8. Lewis Spence, op. cit., p. 77. Spence mentions painted pebbles from the Azilian culture found in Ariege, France. The Abbe Brueil concluded from the markings on these stones that they were objective symbols of the dead, or "soul-houses."

9. H.P. Blavatsky, op. cit., Vol. I, p. 366. Egyptian priests did not eat eggs, sacred to Isis. Buddhists have at all times refrained from eating eggs, says Madam Blavatsky.

10. Ibid., Vol. II, p. 276. A myth from old Cholulu opens with the words, "In the beginning, before the light of the sun had been created . . .

11. Immanuel Velikovsky, *Worlds in Collision*. New York: Pocket Books, 1977, p. 50 et. seq. The author refers to texts and oral traditions from peoples at widely separated places on the earth that tell of the advent of a new sun at the beginning of each new age following some catastrophe.

12. The novitiate would not be entitled to have a Serpent, carved in a high relief spiral, about his staff. Eggs were twined about the staff rod now as the Serpent would be when more spirit power was attained.

12a. Robert Graves, op. cit., p. 263. Graves says that Jeremiah (1 Jeremiah 11) was shown the Menorah, Aaron's almond rod branched and in bud, as a visionary token that God had granted him prophetic wisdom.

13. Pierre Grimal, et al, op. cit., p. 213. Vishnu, as Matsya, the avatar of the fish, saved the world during the Flood, according to Hindu belief.

14. H.P. Blavatsky, op. cit., Vol. I., p. 441. Madam Blavatsky quotes from Confucius: "Divining straws and the tortoise determine good and bad luck." The story of the man who could not find the TCHAY'-TAY-LAITCH, symbol of "good luck," is located here.

15. The frontispiece to Franchino Gafori's *Practica Musicae*, Milan, 1496, depicts the Serpent linking earth with the heavens, presided over by Apollo, the Sun King.

16. See H.W. Janson, op. cit., p. 53, Plate 74.

17. Genesis 22.

18. Genesis 9.

19. Alwyn and Brinley Rees, op. cit., p. 276. The Gandharvas in the

Rig Veda of India were half-man and half-bird; spirits of the air or of the water.

20. Pierre Grimal, et al, op. cit. p. 31. Thoth is portrayed with the head of a sacred ibis.

21. Joseph Campbell, op. cit. pp. 12, 13. Campbell says that, after baptism, early Christian neophytes were drawn from the water like a fish.

CHAPTER FOURTEEN

1. Jennings C. Wise, *The Philosophical History of Civilization.* New York: Philosophical Library, 1955, p. 17 et. seq.

2. Pierre Grimal et al, op. cit., p. 108. The mythical Greek Poseidon, son of Jupiter, was lord of the sea.

3. The *Vancouver Sun*, July 20, 1977. A news item states that in April of 1977, Japanese fishermen caught about two tons of the remains of a strange creature in their nets thirty miles east of Christchurch, New Zealand. Professor Tokio Shakima of Yokahama National University said that the monster was probably a plesiosaur, a fish-eating marine reptile thought to have become extinct about sixty-five million years ago.

4. Revelations 12.

5. H.P. Blavatsky, op. cit., Vol. II, p. 399. Poseidon was sometimes called "God of the Horse."

6. Pierre Grimal et al, op. cit., p. 135. Poseidon's chariot was drawn by creatures half serpent, half horse.

7. Immanuel Velikovsky, op. cit., pp. 163, 164. Velikovsky refers to studies made on the basin of a former body of glacial water called Lake Lahontan, of which the present day Pyramid, Winnemucca, and Walker lakes of Nevada are remnants. Bones of horses, elephants, and camels were found in Lahontan sediments, as well as a spear point of human manufacture. The author also mentions, on page 261, the fact that human artifacts have been unearthed beneath bones of horses and other animals in the Fairbanks district of Alaska.

8. Clarence, son of Basil Joe, and also schooled in his people's lore, said that an account from long ages past tells of a time when aboriginal Sechelt saw a herd of wild horses swimming in and later emerging from the water.

9. Welsh scholar Geoffrey Madoc-Jones, raised in the town of Bethseda, near this lake, says that, after "Marchlyn," "Fawr" is an appositive adjective meaning "great." "March" is Welsh for "steed," and "lyn" means "lake."

10. Jennings C. Wise, op. cit., p. 67 et seq. The "cow" horns of Isis represent the crescent moons, according to this writer.

11. Pierre Grimal et. al., op. cit. p. 142. These forays comprised two of the twelve labours of Hercules.

12. James George Frazer, op. cit. p. 512 and passim.

13. See Pierre Grimal et. al, op. cit., p. 211.
14. Jennings C. Wise, op. cit., pp. 249, 377.
15. Pierre Grimal, et al, op. cit., p. 80.
16. Ibid., plate opposite p. 81.
17. See Homer, *The Odyssey.*
18. Ibid.
19. Genesis 3.
20. Pierre Grimal et al, op. cit., p. 132.
21. See Robert Graves, op. cit., p. 257.
22. Near Prince Rupert, on the northern coast of British Columbia, a full-size likeness of a human being appears deeply indented into a slab of hard sedimentary rock near the beach. Local Tsimshian Indians told Europeans that this figure, referred to now as "The Man Fallen From the Sky," represented their mythical Raven. In Orphic mythology, the raven conducted the candidate into a realm of knowledge beyond death.
23. See Fosco Maraini, op. cit., p. 157. The author says that in China and Japan the Dragon, Turtle, Horse-Giraffe-Unicorn, and Phoenix comprised the Four Spiritual Animals. As well as other creatures of myth and legend, the Sechelt recognized close equivalents to these Spiritual Four. TCHAIN'-KO, Serpent or Dragon, appears still in pictograph form in Salmon Inlet. Likewise, KAY-KAH'-LAH, the Turtle, is outlined in a painting on the shore of Sakinaw Lake. TAH-KAY-WAH'-LAH-KLAHSH, "Horse From the Water," can be seen in natural stone near Chatterbox Falls, Princess Louisa Inlet. While KWAHT-KAY'-AHM, the Thunderbird, did not correspond exactly to the Phoenix, it was a huge bird that existed only in legend. Its stylized likeness can still be found carved into the blades of ceremonial Sechelt paddles.
24. Thomas Crosby, op. cit., p. 99.
25. Cyrus H. Gordon, op. cit., p. 174. Throughout the world says Gordon, there was once a "great common culture" on which all successive cultures drew.
26. The Sechelt began to turn to Christianity in 1862, when a few individuals paddled to New Westminster, where a mission of the Order of Mary Immaculate had been established.
27. James Strange, *Journal.* Madras, 1928.
28. See John Rogers Jewitt, op. cit.